KT-407-645

How to pick a religion

XB00 000012 3545

WOLVERHAMPTON PUBLIC LIBRARIES	
XB000000123545	
Bertrams	14/10/2011
200BAR	£9.99
ALL ✓	01371985

How to pick a religion

A CONSUMER'S GUIDE

TREVOR BARNES

Hodder Education

338 Euston Road, London NW1 3BH.

Hodder Education is an Hachette UK company

First published in UK 2011 by Hodder Education

This edition published 2011.

Copyright © Trevor Barnes 2011

Database right Hodder Education (makers)

All rights reserved. No part of this publication may be reproduced, stored in a retrieval system or transmitted in any form or by any means, electronic, mechanical, photocopying, recording or otherwise, without the prior permission in writing of Hodder Education, or as expressly permitted by law, or under terms agreed with the appropriate reprographic rights organization. Enquiries concerning reproduction outside the scope of the above should be sent to the Rights Department, Hodder Education, at the address above.

You must not circulate this book in any other binding or cover and you must impose this same condition on any acquirer.

British Library Cataloguing in Publication Data: a catalogue record for this title is available from the British Library.

10 9 8 7 6 5 4 3 2 1

The publisher has used its best endeavours to ensure that any website addresses referred to in this book are correct and active at the time of going to press. However, the publisher and the author have no responsibility for the websites and can make no guarantee that a site will remain live or that the content will remain relevant, decent or appropriate.

The publisher has made every effort to mark as such all words which it believes to be trademarks. The publisher should also like to make it clear that the presence of a word in the book, whether marked or unmarked, in no way affects its legal status as a trademark.

Every reasonable effort has been made by the publisher to trace the copyright holders of material in this book. Any errors or omissions should be notified in writing to the publisher, who will endeavour to rectify the situation for any reprints and future editions.

Hachette UK's policy is to use papers that are natural, renewable and recyclable products and made from wood grown in sustainable forests. The logging and manufacturing processes are expected to conform to the environmental regulations of the country of origin.

www.hoddereducation.co.uk

Typeset by Cenveo Publisher Services. Printed in Great Britain by CPI Cox & Wyman, Reading.

Contents

01
Introduction

The spiritual department store

It's often said by the kind of rabbi that combines deep wisdom with a knowing twinkle in the eye that, to be Jewish, you don't have to believe in God – you just have to do what He says. It's a great line with more than a grain of truth in it because, as the aphorism suggests, there are many ways of being a Jew. These range from having a Jewish mother (though in Liberal Judaism just a Jewish father will do the trick) to attending synagogue every Saturday, from studying the Torah and the Talmud night and day to being able to whistle the first four bars of 'My Yiddishe Mama'. The parameters, in other words, are very wide.

The sages of ancient and modern times have wrestled with the question 'Who is a Jew?' and concluded after lengthy debates that so and so is and so and so isn't. The matter seems fixed for several years (even decades and centuries) until a different set of sages comes along with a different take on this perennial conundrum and reaches a different conclusion. Each time, however, many of those deemed not to be Jewish stubbornly assert that they are, and grow irritated by or indifferent to scholarly logic-chopping. In these post-Holocaust times many of them point with bitter exasperation to Nazi Germany and argue that while the rabbis may have been solemnly deliberating about their Jewish status Herr Hitler and his henchmen would have had no such qualms and would have despatched them and their family to the gas chambers regardless. The fact is that, when it comes to laying down the irreducible minimum of requirements for being

Jewish, many things apply and, of these, belief can sometimes be an optional component.

What's more, such an approach applies more often than you'd think to many of the other world religions. Being a non-churchgoing Christian, a nominal Hindu, a less-than-devout Muslim, a lapsed Sikh or a disillusioned Zoroastrian doesn't mean turning your back on everything you have been brought up to celebrate and hold dear. On the contrary, many continue to embrace with great affection the cultural practices they were raised with, even though they may have outgrown some if not all of the key tenets of the faith into which they were born. In short, they might be throwing out the spiritual bathwater but they're determined to hang on to the cultural baby.

And it's those cultural/spiritual packages in all their diversity that this book aims to explore. Let's for a moment imagine we are stepping into a spiritual department store looking for something we think might improve our lives or something that might sit well with our temperament and personality. Let's say we're very much attracted to creativity and the visual arts. Where should we look? Well, certainly to Christianity and to the Bible, which have both provided the raw material for innumerable canvasses reinterpreting the timeless stories of the Old and New Testaments.

It's equally fair to say that Judaism and Islam provide less rich a seam to mine since their historical objections to figurative painting (too much like graven imagery, you see) have dissuaded Jewish and Muslim would-be artists from exercising their artistic potential in this particular way. Depicting the Prophet, for example, and – even more outrageous – the Creator Himself would be blasphemy, whereas to Christian artists of every century the figure of Jesus and that of God seated on His throne in heaven are proper subjects to paint. Not only that, such paintings are to be seen routinely in both galleries and places of worship where their presence is deemed not only appropriate but positively conducive to meditations on the Divine.

Of the eastern religions Japanese and Chinese Buddhism have inspired sublime landscape painting on parchment and silk. The delicate paintings of forests and mountain tops seem to transport you into another realm of reality while animal paintings of frogs or carp are executed with such apparent ease and yet with such precision that they seem to be more frog-like and more carp-like than the real thing. 'Ah,' they seem to be mutely declaring, 'but perhaps the painting of the frog is more real than the real frog in the real pond.' In portraying the essence of the subject they depict, such paintings force us to ask questions about so many things we had hitherto taken for granted. Oh, and they're also exquisitely beautiful.

Shift to a different continent and you'll discover another spiritualized tradition of painting in the canvasses produced by Australian Aborigine artists. Highly prized on the international art market they depict aspects of the natural world that link the sacred landscape of the present with the ancestral past of the tribe, binding the material here-and-now to the spiritualized world that existed at the dawn of human history. For Aborigine peoples the land is the very core of their being and their belief. In their world view the 'Dreamtime' is the primordial period of creation when ancestral creatures roamed the land leaving their physical mark on the Earth in the form of a rock or a cave, a hollow or a river. The paintings that emerge from this tradition are much more than mere decoration. They are said to contain a spiritual power in themselves, embodying as they do the natural, spiritual and moral elements of the created order.

In Hinduism, too, there is evident delight in recreating the spiritual world of the many deities in two, and sometimes three, dimensions. Krishna, perhaps the most popular of the incarnations of the Divine, is frequently pictured herding his cattle or playing with his many female admirers by cool streams and lush pastures. In these he is coloured blue to show that here is no ordinary mortal but the embodiment of an eternal principle. Blue, you see, is the colour of the sky and, hence, infinity. In depicting him as an entity both in and out of time the artwork itself becomes a vehicle for transmitting a spiritual truth.

In Hindu temples the statues of the deities are treated with the reverence due to real people. Like visiting dignitaries and VIPs from the spirit realm they are woken, dressed, fed and ritually put to bed in the evening. When the temple curtains are drawn back at the beginning of religious devotions the god steps into humanity's midst and dwells among the worshippers ... until the curtain is discreetly closed and the emanations of the divine disappear from human view until the next time.

From art to music. If we're of a musical bent we're also likely to be drawn to the choral and instrumental traditions of Christianity. But we might equally head in the direction of Judaism, which has had a rich musical tradition down the ages. Islam, by contrast, has been suspicious of the sensual temptations that the playing of stringed instruments can generate and most of its adherents feel much safer giving music and singing a wide berth.

Switch to architecture, however, and Islam is up there with the greats. Christianity might boast the glories of Durham Cathedral or Notre Dame but Islam can match them with Istanbul's Blue Mosque or the Moorish palace of Granada's Alhambra.

And what else do the various religions offer in the way of meditation and prayer, for example, or family life and sexual equality? If you want to eat well and take delight in the pleasures of the table, to which religious tradition should you look? If social justice and the proper stewardship of the environment are things you hold dear, then which religions will best reflect your concerns? What does each have to say about the afterlife and the rewards we might expect for a good life here on Earth? Similarly which religions hold out the prospect of the greatest punishments for failing to carry out God's commands? Where will you find the most amount of freedom to worship as you choose or, if you think freedom is a dangerous snare, where will you find the most discipline and restraint to keep you on the narrow path of righteousness?

The pages that follow may provide you with an answer. It will be by its very nature partial and one-sided so think of it more as a rough guide to the cultural and intellectual heritage of the world's faiths. When that much-missed comedian and master of the surreal, Spike Milligan, opined that, 'There's a lot of it about', he was not in all probability talking about religion. What he *was* talking about, mind, is anybody's guess. It's fair to say, though, that if he *had* been talking about religion he would have been spot on. As the Americans would say, do the math.

Hinduism reckons to have some 900 million adherents worldwide, Jainism 5 million, Judaism 15 million and Buddhism 375 million. There are an estimated 2 billion Christians worldwide, 1.5 billion Muslims and 23 million Sikhs. This is not including the estimated 6 million Confucians, 4.5 million Taoists and 200,000 Zoroastrians. Add to that the 100 million followers of African traditional religion (Yoruba, Voodoo, Candomblé, Santoría and others), Native American religion and Australian Aborigine spirituality plus the 7 million Baha'is, the 12 million Spiritualists, the 1-million-strong New Age community, the 300 million Animists, Shamanists, Pagans and indigenous believers – not counting the numerous agnostics who haven't made their mind up either way – and you have something like 85 per cent of the planet committed to religious belief in one form or the other.

By any standards this is a very popular department store – one that has grown over time and, as it has added new lines, has spread out over many floors with areas devoted to every conceivable denomination, sect, breakaway faction, splinter group, or otherwise variant of all of the above.

Religion. There's a lot of it about. Read on and decide whether any of it's for you.

Claims and consolations

It is sometimes said that while the claims of religion may be false its consolations are real. As an assertion of fact this is obviously not watertight (reassurance built on falsehood, after all, will console only for so long), but you can see what it's driving at.

Certainty in a perplexing world, the promise of rest for the weary and of justice for the hard-done-by, and the conviction that an eternity of bliss will in due course replace a lifetime of suffering are comforts not to be sniffed at. And whatever else non-believers may rebuke the faithful for it is unlikely to be their peace of mind. True, they may despise what they consider to be their simpleminded credulity but that is another matter altogether. Indeed a fair few of the agnostic persuasion and those of a less militantly atheistic bent are on record as saying they wished that they too were able to believe but that, for one reason or another, they can't. So religion is clearly on to *something*. And whether true or false, it shows no sign of fading quietly away. So what does it have to offer the world?

Well, quite a lot if you listen to its detractors (and any honest look at religion will have to include them in the viewfinder) – intolerance and cruelty for a start. Oh, and bigotry and persecution, not to mention genital mutilation, public execution, jihads, crusades, and lots of really irritating ways of putting a crimp in your free time. The critics have a point. Viewed in a certain light the record of the world's religions is not wholly reassuring. From the dire punishments itemized with such relish in the Hebrew Bible and the Koran to the human sacrifices required to appease the Aztec sun god Huitzilopochtli, religious practices have been historically more, er, demanding than, say, sitting in a draughty church attending to the distant hum of the padre.

Religions have inspired wars and persecutions and do so today. You don't have to look far around the world to find examples of religion at its most dogmatic, exclusive, triumphalist and aggressive. Clutching most of the medals in the Intolerance Olympics right now is probably the provisional wing of the Taliban. And you can see why. In 2010 *Time* magazine published a front-page picture of an 18-year-old Afghan girl who had run away from her abusive in-laws. For the sheer effrontery of this heinous offence (did the Taliban stop to wonder what abuse had driven her to such desperation in the first place?) divine law was invoked and the girl's nose and ears were cut off. Boy, you'd really deserve the gold for that one.

But this particular Olympiad has been running for over four thousand years and the roll call of distinguished medal winners is long and eclectic. European Crusaders held all the top slots in the Middle Ages, with special mention going rightly to the officials and team captains of the various Inquisitions, who terrorized and tortured errant believers in the sure and certain belief that they were saving their eternal souls. Travel further back to Bronze Age Palestine and the biblical account tells of endless slayings and smitings carried out by the Children of Israel on the direct instructions of the Almighty. Little wonder, then, that non-believers are furious and incredulous by turns at the barbarity inflicted in the name of religion and want nothing to do with it.

When the sheer fury has subsided what principally inspires their derision is the faithful's supposed imperviousness to reason. To the non-believer the Bible, the Koran or the Guru Granth Sahib, to take three of the world's holy scriptures, are merely an invitation to the gullible to set aside their powers of rational thought in order to subscribe to all manner of strange and fantastical propositions borne out of a baseless belief in an Almighty. Moses stretching out his hand to summon a plague of locusts on the gathering wind; Jesus turning water into wine and, much later, rising from the dead; Muhammad swept up into the night sky and transported from Mecca to Jerusalem to commune with the Prophets of old; Guru Gobind Singh beheading five of the faithful before miraculously restoring them to full vigour. What sort of implausible fiction is this, the sceptical wonder, and what sort of basis does it provide for erecting any cogent world view?

But if cruelty and fairy tales were all religion had to offer the world surely someone would have twigged much earlier that this was not, all things considered, a great deal. They would have sniffed out the wheeze and rejected it. There must presumably have been a couple of good things thrown into the mix to tempt our distant kin to look up from the fields and start making plans. For sure, in the beginning there was probably a large measure of fear in the mix – the need to placate the terrible gods of fire and thunder, rain and lightning who were believed to regulate the lives of those settling, say, along the fertile banks of the River Indus some 4,500 years ago. But there was probably also a sense of gratitude to someone or something outside themselves that allowed the sun to shine, their crops to ripen and their children to be born. In this interplay between awe and thanksgiving was religion born.

But, scream the sceptics, you don't need an Almighty (or a veritable pantheon of supernatural subordinates) to explain the mysteries of the Universe *any more*. This misguided notion only ever had one virtue; it was the humankind's *first* attempt to explain the pattern and purpose of our lives. But being the first explanation does not make it the best. On the contrary, this first attempt, so the argument goes, was also the worst possible stab at calibrating humanity's place in the *natural* order. It may have been understandable, forgivable even, when set in the context of our primeval ignorance about the way the universe works but now we know about the laws of physics, chemistry and biology there's no excuse for the persistence of such phantasmagorical moonshine. We understand full well the principles of radiation and nuclear fusion these days and they have precious little to do with the Roman god Apollo or the Egyptian sun god Ra. What's more, the residents of Tiverton, say, or Arbroath no longer require the still-beating hearts of captured enemy warriors to be ripped from their chest cavities by Aztec priests on a daily basis to be confident that the sun will rise on time every morning over the village green and the quayside. The Big Bang theory (describing the moment 13 billion years ago when hot matter of infinite density exploded then expanded and cooled to form the beginnings of the universe as we now observe it) has effectively done away with all that.

Ah, but has it? For science tells us only *how*, leaving religion, philosophy, and the imagination to attempt to tell us *why*. Even the most sophisticated measuring techniques can take us back only so far, namely to a split second *after* the Big Bang, not to the moment of explosion itself. And certainly not to any 'moment' before it – if any such prior moment could be said to have existed at all. If *anything* could be said to have existed before it.

'In the beginning...'

So let's attempt an elementary crack at understanding the Big Bang. Let's begin by thinking of the universe as a big empty room. That done, let's imagine the infinitely compressed matter that is about to explode in one gigantic bang as a grenade in the centre of the room. The grenade goes off and, as it detonates, shrapnel is shot out in all directions into that hitherto empty room to fill it with matter that will become the stars and planets we see today. As mega-, giga-, tera-tons of stardust cannon-ball out into space, particles will eventually cool down to form (a mere 9 billion years later) that familiar globe of blue and white we know as planet Earth and potentially everything we see on it today. In other words, it is only a matter of waiting patiently before the elemental plasma spewed out at the beginning of imagined time cools, coagulates and evolves into primitive life forms that over a further 3 billion years will themselves evolve and be reconstituted as Plato, Einstein and the entire celebrity line-up of *Strictly Come Dancing*.

But there is a flaw in this thinking. We are wrong to imagine the pre-Big Bang nothingness as an empty room. Wrong, too, to imagine some sort of celestial grenade exploding into it. One split second before this cataclysmic moment in cosmic history there was nothing. No grenade and, even harder to comprehend, no room. There was *nothing*. Not even empty space. There *was* nothing. *Nothing* existed (or, perhaps, didn't). *Nothing was.* Our world came into being, to use the technical term, *ex nihilo*, to repeat, *from nothing*.

But how are we to get our heads round that? In the face of such unknowables (the religious sensibility would say 'mysteries') the vocabulary of the everyday breaks down and at this point we are left, frankly, to take a punt. Is there a God behind all this or is there not? Secular scientists and humanist philosophers tell us emphatically that there is not and go further by asserting that there doesn't *need* to be one either to understand the world as it is. Believers beg to differ (religious believers, that is, as opposed to secular believers for both positions involve an intellectual leap in the dark or … ahem … an act of faith).

'In the beginning,' the magisterial opening words of the first verse of the King James Bible intone, 'God created the heaven and the earth.' For believers that's the matter settled in one. What was good enough for Moses and the ancient Israelites is good enough for them. God is the eternal reality, they say, and it is God alone who brings the world into existence *ex nihilo* (that phrase again).

Let's stay with the opening words of the Hebrew Bible (the Christian Old Testament) a little longer because, according to the prevailing cosmological theory, they state not just a poetic, metaphorical or philosophical description of Creation but a generally accepted scientific fact. Prior to 1949 when the astronomer and mathematician Fred Hoyle first coined the term 'Big Bang', if you'd asked a scientist how old the universe is and what was there before it came into being, you would have been laughed at for asking a pair of nonsensical questions in the first place. The universe is infinite, you would have been told, the cosmos is eternal – and, of course, always has been. From 1949 onwards that theory was radically revised and to those two questions you will now be told a) about 13 billion years and b) um … not too sure. In other words, we know scientifically that the universe had a beginning and that the opening words of Genesis were spot on in this.

Incidentally, Fred Hoyle may have been credited with a nifty bit of phrase making but the theory to which his 'Big Bang' referred was developed in the 1920s by Georges Lemaître, the Belgian astronomer, and Cambridge, Harvard and MIT-educated cosmologist who posited 'the hypothesis of the primeval atom', aka 'the Cosmic Egg', which, lacking a little something, was to the Big Bang what the belly-go-round and the extruded plastic dingus were to the hoola-hoop. Great theoretical physicist though he undoubtedly was, Lemaître would not perhaps have made a similar splash in the world of Madison Avenue copywriting. Besides, he already had a second (or maybe first) career as a Catholic priest. Atheism, it seems, is not the required qualification for a scientist after all – as the secularists would have us believe. But that is altogether another story.

Interestingly, if we stay with the opening lines of Genesis for one last moment, something quite remarkable happens in the third verse – something neither the redactors of the Hebrew Bible nor its seventeenth-century English translators could have foreseen in their pre-Enlightenment world; religion and twenty-first-century science converging yet again. The third verse reads 'And God said, Let there be light: and there was light.' Now, if you leave out the God stuff, you have the Big Bang in a nutshell. There was nothing. Then 'there was light'. But although the biblical account can encompass the scientific one, the reverse cannot be the case, and so we are, yet again, left contemplating the enduring question. Is there a Prime Mover, a First Cause, a Heavenly Father, a Creator, an Almighty, a *Maker* of Heaven and Earth or not?

The great God debate

If you've picked up this book to find out, then prepare to be disappointed. The last thing it intends to do is even attempt to prove things either way. Rather sharper minds than this writer's have tried – and, of course, failed. As any non-mathematical proof inevitably must. Not that this has prevented the current vogue for staging religio-philosophical sparring matches between proponents of each cause – and even charging an entry fee for the privilege of watching two people doing their best to lasso the wind.

One of the higher-profile encounters involved the former British Prime Minister Tony Blair (red corner, God) stepping into the ring to confront the mighty Christopher Hitchens (blue corner and undefeated heavyweight champion of atheist polemic). It was billed as the clash of the philosophical Titans but in the event turned out to be more like Shirley Temple agreeing to do thirteen rounds with Joe Louis. Great fun but not proof either way. And, even though the Great Hitch floored the Saintly Tony (and by extension the billions of his co-religionists of every hue), he couldn't land a glove on faith itself. Bags of evidence superbly deployed but still no proof. Bags of punch but no knockout blow. A word of sympathy, however, for his doughty contender metaphorically stretched out of the ring after this uneven contest. Even if Tony Blair had brought all the skill of Augustine, Pascal and (to suggest a worthier modern-day opponent) C.S. Lewis, he could not have proved the *existence* of God either. For this, to repeat, is an act of faith. God exists or God does not exist. Those are the only options. It's 50/50. Let's face it, the odds could be worse.

A convenient moment, therefore, to bring in Pascal, Blaise Pascal, the seventeenth-century mathematician and Catholic philosopher who framed the debate more or less in the terms outlined above when he playfully imagined the cosmic choice as a bet.

> *Belief is a wise wager. Granted that faith cannot be proved, what harm will come to you if you gamble on its truth and it proves false? If you gain, you gain all; if you lose, you lose nothing. Wager, then, without hesitation, that He exists.*

However, Pascal couldn't have bargained for a muscular and persuasive rebuttal from (whom else?) Christopher Hitchens interviewed on the BBC's *Newsnight* programme over 300 years later. This wasn't Pascal at his best, Hitchens maintained, and the wager schtick not Pascal's finest hour. But wasn't it reasonable, asked Paxman, in the interests of self-preservation beyond the grave, to lay a bet on God's existence? How could you lose? It was a challenge all the more poignant and possibly all the more urgent in Hitchens's case given the gathering threat of his own mortality following a cancer diagnosis. Tacitly spurning all sympathy and special pleading, emphatically no, it was not reasonable, he averred. Far from it, it was morally pusillanimous and lacked any vestige of intellectual integrity – and he proceeded nobly to explain why.

Far be it from me to traduce the great man but, as I recall, his argument went as follows. Faced with the (admittedly unlikely) possibility of a post-mortem encounter with the Almighty on the Seat of Judgement there would be, Hitchens readily admitted, quite a lot of explaining to do. Clearly wrong-footed by the sudden and unexpected appearance of the Ancient of Days he would be forced to do some quick thinking and persuasive talking – those were, after all, two of the things the Lord had seen fit to equip the earthly Hitch with sixty-odd years earlier. Once recovered from the surprise of the celestial chinwag, Hitchens would go on to explain in all honesty how, on the evidence presented to him in his lifetime and on the strength of his (evidently now God-given) intelligence, he had been simply unable to be swayed by the arguments.

For many of the reasons already listed he would argue that, finding it temperamentally and intellectually impossible to believe in God, he had preferred to leave things that way (at least until such time as more compelling evidence emerged). Far more honourable to do that than to take the easy and ignoble way out of the great God debate by merely closing his eyes and placing a bet on God's existence in the hope of lenient treatment beyond the grave. Sure, he continued, it would be a little embarrassing to have to confront the existence of an entity whose non-existence he had argued for for so long but, all things considered, he was confident he had a good and honourable defence. Hitchens thus hoped that, having been both consistent and conscientious in his atheism, he would be treated with understanding. OK, so he had admittedly got this God business wrong, but how could he have acted otherwise on the strength of the evidence that had been available to him at the time? Hitchens was reasonably confident that this would at least defer the Final Judgement and quite possibly, after a lengthy exchange of paperwork, get him off on a technicality. It's hard not to conclude that it would.

How he would explain his reaction to the prospect of then joining a party where Mother Teresa and Jerry Falwell were among those knocking back the drinks and canapés was not explained.

Before we leave Christopher Hitchens and distinguished fellow atheists such as Richard Dawkins – the evolutionary biologist who has confidently asserted that the whole notion of God is a mere delusion – let us for a moment get our terminology right. While they undoubtedly subscribe to a non-theist position (i.e. dismiss the idea of a personal God who intervenes in human affairs) it is arguably unfair and quite possibly discourteous to call them 'atheists'. By defining them negatively and in opposition to those who take the theist position we perhaps unwittingly declare our hand and appear already to be taking sides in the God debate. Far better to define them in terms of what they do believe rather than in terms of what they do not and thus far better to use the terms 'humanist' or 'naturalist'.

What the humanist believes is that humanity is the measure of all things. We humans can and should work out our morality in this, the only life we have, and should

reject any notion of reward or punishment in a non-provable
hereafter. Naturalists believe much the same, believing this,
our natural world, to be operating by perfectly natural means
that in due course scientific enquiry will explain. Invoking the
idea of a supernatural agency in human affairs, they would
claim, is as otiose as it is demeaning of human potential.
Faced with the charge that they are insensitive to the mystery
and awe of divine Creation they reply that they are indeed in
awe of the beauty and complexity of the natural world but
that such mysteries as exist today will be fully explained by
natural means tomorrow.

Spoilt for choice

All this needs to be said at the outset because this book is
not intended to be a challenge to (still less an attack on) the
secular humanist position. True, it does presuppose that the
reader is at least sympathetic towards the religious world
view even if he or she does not entirely share it. The mere fact
that you are reading this suggests that, if pressed, you might
consider laying your own personal bet with Pascal rather
than with Dawkins. But the book is quite happy for you to
hedge your bet or, having placed it on 7 red, say, to switch it
suddenly to 5 black – or simply leave the casino altogether. It
makes no attempt to persuade, convert or otherwise beat the
drum for religion in general or any world faith in particular.

It will merely attempt to show the options open to you
should you flip the religious coin and choose to look at the
positive side of faith – in addition to all the negatives listed
above. And positives there must surely be, or why would
something like 5 billion people (some 85 per cent of the
human race) subscribe to one form of religious belief or
another?

As we have seen, in religion's house (with due deference
to the Authorized Version of the New Testament) are many
mansions – Hinduism, Jainism, Judaism, Christianity,
Islam, Sikhism, Buddhism, Zoroastrianism, Rastafarianism,
Confucianism, Baha'i, Shinto, Taoism, the indigenous religions
of North and South America, Africa or Australia, Druidry,
Wicca, Shamanism, Neopaganism, Voodoo, Santería, and a

plethora of cults, sects and new religious movements – not to mention the innumerable subsections of them all. They have all taken positions on the three really big questions in life: where did we come from, why are we here, and where are we going? They all have their quirks and peculiarities dictating what we should wear, what we should eat, whom we should mix with, and how we should arrange the details of our private lives. We are told what we may do, what we may not do, and how we should mark the various milestones in our and others' lives.

Some religions (or at least some of their sub-denominations) are more at home with life's duties and responsibilities, seeing existence down here as nothing more than a preparation for a future life up there (one as yet unknown but, paradoxically, described in sometimes alarming detail). For them life is a vale of tears, an illusion (or, as the journalist and late convert to Roman Catholicism Malcolm Muggeridge once put it, 'a night in a cheap hotel'). Life, you might say, as the eliminating heats for eternity's 1,000 metres. Others see religion as very much a this-worldly pursuit and life as the only show in town. For these, goodness is its own reward and virtue is to be practised for its own sake in the here and now rather than as a down payment on an afterlife.

Some tell you to shave your head; others tell you never to cut your hair in a lifetime. Some tell you to be quiet and contemplate in silence; others tell you to make a joyful noise. Some tell you to go forth and multiply; others to tie a knot in it. So can they all be valid? Or is there one true religion hiding in a barrelful of phonies? To be sure, there is no shortage of religions telling the faithful (or the merely curious) just that – that they are the one true way to salvation and that the other several billion have simply got it wrong. There are many others, however, that diffidently affirm that there are many ways to God and that all of them are equally valid.

But even the isolationists would (perhaps grudgingly) be forced to admit that at the heart of each living faith is an unbreakable link with all the others; the principle of mutuality, of reciprocity, of interdependence. 'Do not hurt others with that which hurts yourself' is how the Buddha is quoted as expressing the principle. The Talmud (the codification of Jewish law) states, 'That which is hateful to you, do not do to your neighbour. That is the whole of the law. The rest is explanation.' Jains assert that 'Just as pain is not agreeable to you, so it is with others. Knowing this principle of equality treat others with respect and compassion.' The precept 'that which you want for yourself, seek for mankind' is attributed to Muhammad while Confucius wrote 'Never impose on others what you would not choose for yourself', and in the New Testament of the Bible Luke records that, in answer to the lawyer asking how he would inherit eternal life, Jesus replied, 'Thou shalt love the Lord thy God with all thy heart and with all thy soul and with all thy strength and with all thy mind, and thy neighbour as thyself.'

The Chief Rabbi once said to me (and, believe me, I've been waiting fifty years to say that) that Judaism is the language God uses to talk to Jews. Subscribe to that generous assertion and you accept Hinduism to be Brahman's chosen language for Hindus, Islam to be Allah's chosen language for Muslims, and Zoroastrianism to be Ahura Mazda's chosen language for Zoroastrians. You get the drift. No competition, no threat, no punch-ups.

So just imagine for a moment that the world's religions are spread before you waiting for you to select one. Which one will it be? Which one corresponds to your particular temperament? You're looking for peace, quiet and reflection. So where should you go? Or perhaps you'd prefer a full-throated, noisy celebration of faith. Where then is it best to look? You like the idea of a religion that can express its world view on canvas or in stone or in any other of the many artistic outlets the human hand and mind are capable of devising. Which religions allow you to do that best? Which allow you to play your guitar and which would rather you did not? Which best square with your scientific temperament, which best correspond to your concerns about the environment, and what do they all have to say about your family and social life?

Stepping into the department store of religions you will find many products on many levels. There will be exotic new lines and countless special offers – alongside own-brand variants of the same basic commodities (Creation, afterlife, good and evil, etc. etc.). But if you have a special purchase in mind, in which direction should you head to stock up on social justice, art and creativity, contemplation and meditation, doubt, authority, freedom and restraint, and what will you find on the floors marked 'sex', 'money', 'power', 'business' and 'recreation'?

Remember that some brands have been around for an awfully long time and survived virtually unchanged. Others have had to be repackaged to make them more popular with a changing clientele. And one or two have been withdrawn altogether through lack of demand – though they can, with prior notice, be ordered in. Remember, too, that the stock is constantly changing and, as the manager will tell you, you never can tell what to expect in tomorrow's delivery. Here is a store guide. It's not exhaustive but it's a start. And there's no obligation to buy.

02

Art and architecture

From the high renaissance to the mists of prehistory

The next time you're in the Vatican (oh, all right then, just Google it) take a look at Michelangelo's *Pietà*, his sculpture of the Virgin Mary holding the dead Christ on her lap and staring at her lifeless son with the sorrow and infinite pity of a mother bereaved. But look a little longer and ask yourself why, inexplicably, there seems to be something not quite right about the marble figures in front of you.

There is sorrow, to be sure, and there is pity (the *pietà* of the Italian title). But strangely absent is the raw emotion of a woman cradling a tortured son. You have doubtless seen such bereavements on TV in news reports from Gaza and Jerusalem, from Baghdad and Kabul, but when did you last see such grace and serene acceptance on the face of a grieving mother only moments after her son's violent death at the hands of foreign oppressors?

Moreover if Christ is traditionally thought to have been 33 at the time of his crucifixion, then his mother must have been at least in her late 40s when the terrible events depicted here took place. Look again. You will search in vain for a middle-aged mother and see only the radiant young woman visited 34 years earlier by the Angel Gabriel. This is all wrong. Michelangelo must have got his wires crossed. He was only a young lad of 24, after all – 24 for goodness' sake! – when he executed this and clearly had a lot to learn. Clearly he has sculpted the Virgin of the Annunciation not the ageing Mary of the Crucifixion and nobody has had the nerve to tell him. Very touchy, these artists.

But that's not all. Look at the supposedly 'lifeless' Christ and do you not see a vibrant musculature still pulsing with blood and breath, the right arm still elastic and the legs unaccountably defying the inexorable gravity of death?

So either Michelangelo was, in fact, pretty useless as an artist or he was doing all this deliberately for a desired effect. Giving him the benefit of the doubt, we realize that the desired effect, in short, is to tell a story through these two figures amounting to more than merely the sum of the sculpture's individual parts. This is not just a depiction of a woman and her dead son. It is, in essence, an allegory of the entire Christian story.

Michelangelo has taken the decision to imbue Mary with the spiritual and moral purity that set her apart from other women all those years ago, a purity that made her, in God's eyes, a suitable vessel to bear His only son. In ignoring her chronological age in favour of her ageless inner beauty he allows us to register the sadness of the event but to go beyond it. Through her eyes we see that the story is not over, that Christ will indeed rise from the dead to redeem the world from sin. And, sure enough, are we not almost witnessing the first stirrings of this world-changing event when we look at the strangely chiselled posture of her son? Christ has died, but is he really dead? Is this but a slumber from which he will soon awake cradled in his mother's arms as he was at birth? In these two figures we have both humanity and transcendence; birth, death and resurrection with the attendant promise of an immeasurable love that will one day wash away all tears.

What a work of art and what a story. And both of them only possible thanks to one of the three great world monotheistic religions – Christianity.

Oh, yes, you might have to sit through a few bottom-numbing sermons in draughty churches, you might have to bite your lip as priests, bishops, popes and people who should know better argue over the minutiae of the faith rather than get on with the job of healing the sick and comforting the dying but, goodness, it must be some consolation knowing that your faith holds the key to understanding and appreciating some of the best works of art the human race has ever produced.

And it doesn't stop with the *Pietà*, for Michelangelo is only one of the giants of canvas and stone who have reinterpreted the Bible stories in the most dramatic and arresting ways.

Think of Renaissance painters such as Fra Angelico, Leonardo, Raphael or Mantegna (and, by the way, if you want to see in paint what the dead weight of a lifeless corpse *really* looks like, look no further than Mantegna's *Dead Christ*). Think of the schools that produced Bellini, Titian, Tintoretto, El Greco, Caravaggio or Bernini. Call these giants to mind and marvel at the power the Christian story has had on some of the greatest artists in human history.

Of course, you don't have to be a Christian to understand or enjoy such works of art but, if you're thinking of joining a religious tradition into which the plastic arts have been hard-wired for centuries if not millennia, then you could do worse than hitch your wagon to the Christian star. You may find the happy-clappy style of some Evangelical worship a little too simplistic for your taste, you may find Anglo- and Roman Catholic services too remote and ritualized, but wander round any half-decent art gallery (not to mention London's National Gallery, the Prado or the Louvre) and you'll encounter life-enhancing images of the Christian story that will retain their power for as long as pictures are looked at.

Sister Wendy Beckett (b. 1930), Christian contemplative and art critic

You must remember the difference between Christianity and other religions is that Christianity is based wholly on Jesus and Jesus was God and Man. And once you have 'and man' you can make an image. You cannot make an image of God. So the Jews and Muslims have nothing to portray. Their God never takes a human form. This is an exception. It happened just once in the whole history of the world. And once it had happened then imagery followed.

Remember that God is the supreme **beauty** *and delighting in the beautiful things that His children have made is*

*something that should be dear to all of us. What we learn
from painting is the **wonder** of creativity. So I get very
great pleasure from looking at these dreams, these images,
these visions called forth into the materiality of paint by the
greatest among our brothers and sisters.*

*I think if someone came to me and said, 'I have no religion
and I'd like to have one. Give me a steer', I wouldn't bring
in anything to do with art. I would say you should look into
your heart and ask what is it you need. I would say if you
need a strong and simple structure, you should investigate
Catholicism, which, like all religions, is not an end but a
means. So I would suggest that you **read the Gospels,** think
about Jesus and if you begin to understand that he could
fulfil a need of your heart and add meaning to your life that
is based upon his **self-giving,** then go and get instruction.*

*I remember filming a series in Amsterdam and one of the
crew, a young man, asked me if I would go for an early-
morning walk with him along the canal. And he said, 'You
know I haven't got a religion and I'm perfectly happy with
that. Is there anything wrong with me?' And I said, 'No.
No. If God wants you to have a religion, you'll feel the need.
Until you feel the need, just go on trying to **be a good man**.*

Christian art has an honourable and ancient pedigree. The
impulse to reproduce moving objects on static surfaces is almost
as old as humankind itself. In the very earliest days of our
evolution, of course, the need merely to survive took precedence
over hobbies so for several thousand years our distant kin left no
permanent trace of their all too transitory lives. All that changed,
however, as soon as the first hunter-gatherers felt secure
enough to put their feet up after a long day's foraging and used
their down time to adorn their surroundings with miniature
representations of the world around them.

Our palaeolithic ancestors at Lascaux in south-west
France or Altamira in northern Spain produced perhaps
the best-known examples of cave art when they created a
truly stunning series of cave paintings of deer, bison and
wild boar. It seems possible that these images were used

in a ritualistic way, perhaps as part of some religious rite to ensure a constant supply of food, perhaps as a totemic yearning for dominion and belonging. We shall never know for certain, for, in the absence of written records, all is speculation. But it seems reasonable to conclude that, while the art is not always driven by religion, the two spring from a common source.

Olympus and Sinai

You'll be hard pressed these days to find a religious group dedicated to the worship of Zeus, Poseidon or Apollo (or indeed of any of the other gods and goddesses of the ancient Greeks and Romans) but look around at what those civilizations left behind them and you might start wishing you could. Take the Parthenon, for instance, the ancient Greek temple to the goddess Athena. The purity of its form, the geometric sophistication of its design, and the integrity of its construction on an outcrop of rock dominating the city of Athens all conspire to put religious worship – and, for the ancient Greeks, the ensuing virtues of beauty, order, democracy and civilization itself – at the centre of public life. The Acropolis. or 'Citadel', with its cluster of sanctuaries, temples, altars, theatres and sacred spaces represents arguably the high point of classical civilization when the sacred and the civic came together in one sublime and unified whole.

Such values persisted but were refashioned by the artists, architects and engineers of ancient Rome who similarly could produce buildings both sacred and profane. Look how easily the Pantheon (the temple 'to all the Gods') sits alongside that monument to both human depravity and civil engineering, the Colosseum.

When, in the early fourth century CE, the Emperor Constantine decreed that Christians should no longer be persecuted in the Empire and subsequently established Christianity as the state religion, he allowed the cult that had flourished largely in secret to come out into the open and speak its name. Christian art was on its way. But why was Judaism, which after all predated Christianity by a millennium and a half, not keeping pace?

The answer lies on the summit of Mount Sinai where Moses had received ten clear instructions. Among them these from Exodus 20:1–4:

> And God spake all these words, saying. I am the Lord thy God, which have brought thee out of the land of Egypt, out of the house of bondage. Thou shalt have no other gods before me. Thou shalt not make unto thee any graven image, or any likeness of any thing that is in heaven above, or that is in the earth beneath, or that is in the water under the earth.

This is by any standards fairly clear and straightforward. And for good measure verse 23 states unequivocally:

> Ye shalt not make with me gods of silver, neither shall ye make unto you gods of gold.

Indeed, it was so clear to the rabbis of old that they ruled that pious Jews should not look on coins engraved with the heads of Roman emperors. Not least because, in many cases, the emperors saw themselves as gods and were revered as such in everyday life. Such injunctions against idolatry have cast a long shadow and one that Jewish artists have been working under for generations since.

In time, Christianity came to accept that art could be used positively, both for the instruction of the unlettered and as a way of beautifying places of worship. As such, painting became an expression of devotion rather than a focus of worship. Many Jews remained unconvinced and looked with horror as the medieval Church not only sanctioned religious art but commissioned pieces that regularly depicted Jesus, Mary, the apostles and the saints. While the walls of their synagogues were free of artistic representation, Christian churches and cathedrals were chock-full of it. How could anyone worship God, they wondered, with such temptations and distractions? They concluded that worship of the One True God was impossible under such circumstances and that Christianity's fondness for representational art was evidence of a relapse into pagan idolatry.

So persistent have these attitudes been down the ages that the art critic Jackie Wullschlager has wondered whether there can be said to be such a thing as Jewish art at all. Are Modigliani's paintings Jewish? In what sense are Lucian Freud and Mark Rothko 'Jewish painters'? Does the architect, artist, musician and all-round cultural polymath Daniel Libeskind design Jewish buildings? Wullschlager herself was not the first to be aware of the pitfalls of answering either way and reminds us that the last person able to answer such questions definitely was Adolf Hitler.

Look at Marc Chagall's work, however, and things become perhaps a little clearer. First, the paintings. Not all obviously Jewish, to be sure, but with enough prayer shawls, rabbis, angelic emanations and studies of east European shtetls to make a Jewish influence unmistakeable. Couple this with what he said about his own formation, 'If I were not a Jew I would not be an artist', and it's game, set and match for those maintaining there is such a thing as Jewish art. But compared to the sheer numbers of Christian painters over the years such painters are rare.

Alongside Chagall one could mention Soutine, Nussbaum, Man Ray, Mark Gertler, El Lissitsky, Ron Kitaj and more, but one is still left wondering why a painting of Solomon and the Queen of Sheba or of Belshazzar's Feast couldn't have been painted by a Jewish Piero della Francesca or a Jewish Rembrandt. After all they would have had the entire Hebrew Bible as their inexhaustible subject matter. One's left to muse wistfully on what might have happened if the injunction on graven imagery had not been so complete – and, possibly more to the point, on what Jewish artists might have created had they not had to battle with two millennia of anti-Semitism that confined them to a few fixed trades and tacitly warned them off achieving too much prominence in an overwhelmingly Christian world. Either way, we are immeasurably the poorer and it will not be Judaism that the seeker will choose should he or she be looking for an artistic heritage. Yes, there are beautiful artefacts – spice towers, candelabra, silverware, glassware, jewellery – and there are fine examples of synagogue architecture and sacred calligraphy but the sad fact remains that Judaism does not yet have a Leonardo.

Depicting the unseen

Islam has taken a similarly hard-line view of the plastic arts, allowing only abstract patterns to decorate their mosques. Repeating designs (often called arabesques in the Western world) served to suggest the infinite and the eternal and were thought to be suitable ornamentation for buildings with an ultimately transcendent purpose. Such patterns found their way into other artefacts such as silverware, pottery and, pre-eminently, carpets where weavers would often introduce a deliberate mistake into the otherwise regular design as if to suggest that God alone is perfect and mere mortals cannot hope to emulate the perfection of the divine hand.

Even where human representation has appeared in an Islamic context – in book and manuscript illumination, for example, or in the Mughal miniatures of northern India in the sixteenth century CE – there has been an absolute prohibition on depicting the face of the Prophet Muhammad. On the rare occasions he does appear, his face is left blank or wholly obscured by a white veil.

As a result of this widespread prohibition of representational art Islam, like Judaism, has produced no canvasses to match those of Christian artists down the ages. It has, however, excelled in sacred architecture and produced buildings every bit the equal of its Christian counterparts. Who could fail, for example, to include the Shah Abbas Mosque in Isfahan in Iran among the most impressive places of worship in the world? Or the mausoleum of India's Taj Mahal as one of the most serene and architecturally perfect of any structure created by human mind and hand?

In recent times more militantly conservative strains of Islam have argued against representational art of any kind. They have even, it sometimes appears, taken against conventional notions of beauty itself if that beauty is not of a spiritual nature in general and of an Islamic nature in particular. Hence in 2001 two magnificent statues of the Buddha that had been carved into the rock of the Bamiyan Valley of central Afghanistan 1,500 years ago were intentionally destroyed by dynamite by the Taliban on the grounds that they were idols and deemed blasphemous. Openly deriding world opinion, they thus systematically reduced to non-existence one of the glories of the Buddhist world and at a stroke transformed a UNESCO World Heritage Site into a pile of rubble. The world reacted with justifiable permutations of anger, disbelief and sadness, concluding that, whatever else the Taliban are, art lovers they are not.

But the rich cultural and artistic heritage of Islam isn't to be dismissed so lightly – even by a group of philistine extremists who would claim art can only distract the viewer from the real focus of life, which is God. But they have seriously missed the point, as Muslim scholars will affirm. Art, on the contrary, can be used to strengthen the spiritual life. Travel back in time eight centuries to the Ghaznavid gardens and palaces of Afghanistan itself, for example, and you would see terraces, courtyards, carvings and a cultural landscape that would remind believers of the world to come. For Islamic art at its various high points, in contrast to western art, which is largely representational, has been devotional in character, pointing towards the beauty and perfection of Creation and, above all, expressing a relationship with the invisible and ineffable Allah. The beauty of Islamic art lies not within the outer shell – wonderful though the natural and man-made world can be – but in the inner core of the heart and the spirit. In short, if you're thinking about exploring the riches of the Islamic artistic tradition, you will be richly rewarded.

Eastern religious art

Hinduism's artistic traditions are similarly rich but distinctively non-western. Among the 64 *kalas*, or traditional Hindu arts, listed in *A Dictionary of Hinduism* you will find such pursuits as mosaic tiling, painting, making flower garlands, sewing, perfumery, costume decoration, beverage preparation, and furniture caning, alongside personal grooming, splashing and squirting with water (SIC), and even tongue twisters and training parrots and mynas to speak. Though difficult perhaps to appreciate as art in the western sense these folk skills are woven into

Hindu life and seen as everyday expressions of the divine plan for human kind.

Hinduism's conventional representational art tends to depict scenes from its sacred texts such as the heroic deeds of Krishna and Arjuna on the field of battle from the Bhagavad Gita. All are technically accomplished but their primary colours and stylistic uniformity often seem to lack the subtlety of much western (Christian) figurative art. Similarly many Sikh representations of the gurus and saints, equally skilful in execution, seem less nuanced than the best of their Christian counterparts. However, when looked at through the eyes of faith, representations of, say, Krishna on a riverbank or Guru Nanak singing hymns with his companions go beyond the merely aesthetic and enter into the realm of devotion.

If you're considering the Buddhist pathway of spirituality, you won't be disappointed by the artistic treasures you'll encounter. While beautiful to look at, Buddhist-inspired art also has an extra quality that transcends the merely technical and aesthetic. And, as we shall see, with one exception, the tradition is markedly different in intention from the representational schools of the west.

Buddhism arrived in China around the second century BCE and by the time of the European Renaissance had permeated Chinese art. In particular, it gave painters an honoured place in society and saw their work as an essential element in meditation practices. While some monks might spend hours meditating on a single word or even a syllable, others might choose an aspect of the natural world – a flower, a pond or a mountain, say. When artists began to paint the natural world around them they were involved in a similar process, capturing the essence of a landscape and trying to capture on silk or parchment the inner meaning of what they saw. As such, a moonlit landscape by Ma Yuan around the thirteenth century CE, for example, becomes a practical aid to meditation. These silk scrolls were often stored in elaborate containers as proof of their worth and taken out for monks and other Buddhist practitioners to use as a starting point for their reflections.

Perhaps the nearest thing they resemble in the Christian tradition is the devotional icon, which is painted in a focused and reverential state of mind in order to evoke religious sentiments in the viewer. While not the object of worship, it thus becomes an aid to devotion, aiming to create a mood within which worship can take place. Similarly when Buddhist artists used pen and ink or brush and ink to draw pine trees in a forest, or a mountainside in the mist, or fish in a pond, they, too, would meditate on the view and recreate the inner meaning of the landscape in the finished image. Although the lines are confident and assured, they are also drawn with the utmost delicacy. Detail is kept to a minimum as if the eye is being constantly directed not so much to the thing itself as to an essential reality beyond the mere image.

Buddhism was also responsible for shaping Japanese artistic traditions from the seventh century onwards. It has been said that the principal difference between eastern art and western is that eastern art depicts the spirit and western art depicts the form. Nowhere does this observation apply better than to Zen Buddhist art. Whether in calligraphy, in ceramics or in painting the artist is producing his or her work in a meditative state and aims to transmit that state of mind into the characters, the pot or the painting.

Zen Buddhism is perhaps most renowned, in the west at least, for producing masterpieces of landscape art. If you are drawn to the stillness and intensity of the Buddhist experience, you will almost certainly find the Zen gardens of Japan among the most beautiful and sublime creations on Earth. Not for nothing is the Ryoan-ji Temple in Kyoto considered a World Heritage Site. Its dry stone garden is both its focus and its crowning glory.

This 30-by-10-metre rectangle contains neither flowers nor trees, neither shrubs nor ponds. It is a plain area of white raked gravel dotted with 15 rocks arranged with tantalizing precision so that only 14 can be seen from any one point. It is said that only when you have attained spiritual enlightenment will you be able to see the last invisible stone. It's gardening, Jim, but not as we know it. If it's simplicity, serenity and ageless beauty you hanker after, then Zen Buddhist art is definitely for you.

Move a continent away to Australia and you may find the native Aborigine spirituality exerts a powerful attraction – particularly to the western city dweller yearning for a closer relationship with the land. Aborigine art certainly reflects that and taps into an ancient culture of sacred storytelling that informs every aspect of Aborigine life. For the Aborigine people every aspect of the natural landscape is sacred – every rock, every hollow, every mountain, every creek. The indentations of the landscape not only hark back to the primeval era of the 'Dreaming' but owe their very existence to ancestral beings who roamed the Earth and literally left their footprints on the land that have become the features we see today.

Aborigine art uses a wide variety of symbols – dots that may be raindrops or stars or sparks, wavy lines that may represent ripples or snakes or running water, curves that may be clouds or wind or storms. Non-representational in nature these artworks seem nonetheless to have a distant kinship with the palaeolithic pictograms of Lascaux and Altamira. Both forms seem to be reaching beyond the here and now but, whereas our earliest ancestors drew their subject matter from the world they could see all around them, Aborigine artists seem to be using their mind's eye to conceptualize the beauty of Creation. In this sense Aborigine art is both age-old and intensely modern at the same time – intensely collectible, too, as art lovers the world over have realized. And, to end on a mercantile and distinctly unspiritual note, if you're drawn to the Aborigine world view and to its art, then buying a few canvasses (if you can afford them) will prove to be a shrewd investment. They are currently fetching high prices on the international art market – though whether the financial reward you will reap will be worth more than the spiritual benefit you derive will, of course, be up to you and your conscience to decide. But happy hunting.

1 Displaying a distinctly western bias, **Christianity** occupies the top slot for the variety, subtlety and depth of its representational tradition of painting. When a simple story, the Parable of the Prodigal Son, for example, can be rendered in a few simple pen strokes by a genius like Rembrandt and reduce the viewer to tears, you know you are in the presence of twofold genius: the genius of the artist who can take a primal tale and invest it with overwhelming emotion and humanity, and the genius of the story itself, drawn as it is from a religion that claims to have emerged from nothing less than the intersection of the temporal and the eternal. God made flesh, the flesh made word, and the word rendered unforgettable in paint and stone, ink and wood.

2 **Islam** for the elaborate simplicity and transcendence of its architecture. Gaze on Isfahan's Imam Mosque in Iran and feel your breath being taken away.

3 Chinese and Japanese **Buddhism** for their nature paintings that use representation to go beyond representation. The fine tracery of their lines contains both delicacy and power and points towards the ultimate reality that lies behind the most mundane of everyday objects. Things of beauty, joys for ever.

03

Music

Art thou troubled?

Who knows when the first stringed instrument was plucked and the first wind instrument blown? Who knows what the first musical performances sounded like and with what excitement, joy or alarm they were received?

And, aside from the 'when' and the 'what', there's the tantalizing lure of the 'why'. Was music conjured up into being to reply to the low moan of the wind across the mouth of a cave at nightfall or to copy and tame the whistling gale heard on a barren heath? Was music designed to recreate the soothing sound of summer birdsong in the depths of winter or did it explode spontaneously to accompany nascent vocal harmonies round an evening fire? Ask on, for we know not – save to surmise with a fair degree of confidence that it was in response to something that has always lain deep, deep within us all.

Music, as Handel rightly knew, calms us when we are troubled. It entertains us when we are happy, and quite often it takes us outside ourselves to a new dimension of awareness when we least expect it. Entertainment aside, that's just what religion does. So it's hardly surprising that there's an overlap between the two. But if you're musical yourself or just have an appreciation of this most allusive of all the arts, which religion should you pick to indulge your talent or satisfy your desire?

Living traditions and vanished harmonies

The oldest unbroken tradition of sacred music is to be found in Hinduism so, if you're looking for something with a lengthy pedigree, this is a good place to start – and maybe end – your quest. Archaeological excavations at Harappa and Mohenjo-Daro near the cities of Lahore and Hyderabad in modern-day Pakistan have unearthed the remains of flutes and stringed instruments. Here, at these major centres of the early Indus civilization, therefore, is evidence of a musical tradition dating back more than five thousand years.

What these age-old melodies sounded like can only be guessed at from the echo they may have left in the classical music of northern India and in the so-called Carnatic music of the south. In Tamil Nadu's capital city, Chennai (formerly Madras), is to be found the largest concentration of Carnatic musicians in the world. Head for Chennai's six-week-long music season in December if you want to get a flavour of the musical forms that have been developing within this civilization for five millennia and more. And thrill to the exciting ragas or melodic modes of Indian classical music and to the hymns and the ritual chanting.

But don't take my word for it. Listen to some of the Vedic chants yourself (the Gayatri Ganapatha is as good a place as any to start) and experience the power of these oral incantations taken from Hinduism's oldest scriptures, the Vedas. Lost in a quasi-hypnotic trance of sacred harmonies you'll then begin to realize why the United Nations Educational, Scientific and Cultural Organization (UNESCO) declared Vedic recitation to be masterpieces of 'the oral and intangible heritage of humanity'. It's a grand title but one that's appropriate to such an otherworldly sound.

Little wonder that these tantalizingly repetitive but mathematically sequenced musical forms can go on for hours, with different ragas suited to different times of the day or night and to the different seasons such as that of the approaching monsoon. Concert performances, with perhaps one vocalist and a small ensemble of instruments including sitar, tabla and harmonium, thus become religious experiences in which you are surrounded and transported by sounds that will take you back into the shared history of humankind – and, it's hoped, into a higher level of consciousness. A congregation from the Home Counties rising stiffly from the pews to knock out half a dozen verses from Hymns Ancient and Modern, it is emphatically not.

Becoming a Jain or a Sikh will secure you entry into a similar sort of musical universe. *Kirtan* (from the Sanskrit 'to repeat') are the familiar repetitive hymns of Sikh devotion while *mantras* (also popular in Buddhist practice) take a single syllable, word or group of words and repeat it to create a spiritual transformation within the individual. In this way, the very sound itself is imbued with divine power.

Perhaps the chief and most sacred single syllable in the Hindu lexicon is the mystical Om or Aum (meaning simply 'yes') whose very utterance is said to elevate the sayer into direct communion with the divine. This is not chanting as entertainment but as participation in the primal harmony of Creation – and, it's believed, the nearest a human being will come to hearing the divine sounds that breathed the cosmos into life.

It's music, Jim. But not as we know it.

Of course, not all Sikhs and Hindus can sustain this level of intensity all the time, so inevitably more popular, folk versions of the basic melodies have emerged. One of the best known and popular of these styles in the west is bhangra, an energetic toe-tapping form of music and dance originating in Punjabi culture to celebrate the incoming harvest. Nowadays, though, from Bradford to west London you won't need to know an ear of corn from a hole in the ground to be able to enjoy the vibrant bhangra beat so beloved of film soundtracks and Asian pop videos. You'll also encounter it during the latter half of Hindu and Sikh weddings at the communal reception where the older generation bows to the inevitable and admits that this form of new-fangled secular(ish) music, while not always to their taste, is not so hard on the ear after all – and may be the price they'll have to pay to ensure the younger generation retains its attachment to community worship and culture.

Buddhist and Shinto musical forms are not always easy on the western ear. Even the chants of Japanese Buddhism's Soka Gakkai movement, popular among western devotees at the moment, rely on a guttural, raw-sounding technique of throat-singing that is generally alien to western traditions but which sounds undeniably powerful when heard at full volume.

Shomyo chants used in Shintoism are structured around a basic pentatonic (five-note) scale without semitones and, as melodies, sound simple to the uninitiated. Likewise, the *gagaku*, or elegant instrumental and vocal traditions of the Imperial court, will sound a bit strange to you if you've been brought up with western popular music as your background wallpaper.

However, if you're interested in percussion then Japanese *taiko* will almost certainly be for you. This has been part of folk and classical musical traditions for generations but has developed into a percussive art form of its own, functioning both as ceremonial accompaniment and as popular entertainment. The next time the Kodo Ensemble of drummers is in town, go along and listen to them, noting (as if you could possibly miss it) the *odaiko*, or 'large drum', which, at some 12 feet in diameter, is the largest drum in the world and requires the performer to be strapped onto a special raised seat to play it. The whole performance is expressive and exciting and is presented very much as a secular spectacle.

Temple, synagogue and concert platform

It is known that music played a large part in early Jewish religion – King David himself is celebrated as a musician and composer and traditionally said to be the author of the Psalms. What's not clear is whether these sacred songs were originally accompanied by a harp, though certainly Psalm 150 refers to instruments of praise including the trumpet, harp, tambourine, lyre, organ and cymbals. What is likely, though, is that these were used in temple ritual.

Following the destruction of the Temple and the exile, worship took place in the home and at the synagogue, where over time the instrumental musical tradition declined and the ritual came to revolve around unaccompanied vocal renditions of prayers and texts such as the Kaddish and Kol Nidre performed by a trained and designated cantor.

How much opportunity you'll have to put your own musical talents into practice will largely depend on the branch of Judaism you choose. Orthodox synagogues tend not to use instruments and rely on an unaccompanied cantor to provide the haunting refrains, aching lamentations, and the Psalms of joy and belonging so typical of Jewish sacred music. Progressive synagogues often have an organ to accompany the cantor and the congregation and see no reason not to have mixed choirs. From time to time they might import more instruments for special occasions.

But if you're expecting the Jewish musical tradition you hope to be joining to be predominantly liturgical and rather conservative in flavour, think again. Outside the synagogue Jewish community life is suffused with music of every kind. There's klezmer, the instrumental dance music with its rising and swooping clarinet, its urgent percussive accordion and its plaintive fiddle; there's folk music and there's classical. In short, everything to make a party, a bar or bat mitzvah, or a wedding go with a swing.

Secular Jewish music, of course, is still Jewish music and it sometimes seems that string playing is hard-wired into it. Look at some of the major performers – from Itzhak Perlman to the late Yehudi Menuhin, from Pinchas Zukerman to the late Jascha Heifetz – and you'll appreciate that the number of virtuoso performers is entirely disproportionate to the size of the Jewish population. The religion is awash with world-class pianists such as Daniel Barenboim, Peter Frankl and Vladimir Ashkenazy, or world-class conductors such as James Levine, André Previn and Lorin Maazel. Look at its list of classical composers – Leonard Bernstein, Aaron Copland, George Gershwin, Steve Reich, Philip Glass, not to mention legendary songwriters such as Bob Dylan, Irving Berlin, Randy Newman, Neil Diamond, Paul Simon and so on, and you get the idea.

Becoming a Jew is a smart move if you're musically inclined because music is in the Jewish DNA.

Church and cathedral

The Christian musical tradition is more than a match, however, and can take on all comers in terms of aesthetics, quality, variety and range of the music, levels of technical sophistication, and even availability and cost.

So if you're attracted to Christianity as a religious option you'll be plugging yourself into arguably the richest musical tradition in the history of civilization. Let's go for a quick canter through it.

The earliest written forms were Gregorian chant, a single line of mellifluous and undulating melody sung solo or in unison, and associated with specific religious texts. They were often used by religious orders of monks and nuns but you can easily find choirs outside the cloisters today who will welcome your participation. Moreover, these melodies also underpin most Christian music written from the Middle Ages until the present day.

As polyphony – the blending of two or more independent melodic lines – developed throughout the Middle Ages, complex and intricate musical forms emerged under composers such as Machaut, Dufay and Josquin, whose choral musical compositions or motets and settings for the Mass became the jewels of the medieval and Renaissance canon. The next great flowering sees the rise of truly sublime composers such as Palestrina (*Missa Papae Marcelli*), Tallis (the 40-part motet *Spem in Alium*), Byrd (Mass settings for three, four or five voices), and Victoria (*Tenebrae Responsories*). Tudor England tops those with equally high-quality music in the form of Sheppard, Gibbons, Weelkes and many more.

The Baroque period sees the development of larger-scale instrumental works including Monteverdi's setting of the Vespers, and the Vivaldi and Bach choral works. It is Bach (as popular today as ever) whom you'll have to thank for producing some of the greatest masterpieces of religious music. His *St Matthew Passion*, *St John Passion* and the great setting of the Mass in B minor for choir, soloists and orchestra are unsurpassable. Don't forget Handel's genius, either, or his role in developing religious oratorios such as *Messiah*, *Israel in Egypt* and *Solomon*.

Then we come to the Classical period with Mass and Requiem settings on a courtly scale by Mozart and Haydn for choirs, soloists and orchestra. Then the enormous *Missa Solemnis* by Beethoven (which is the religious equivalent of his Ninth Symphony).

The development of the dramatic oratorio continues through the Romantic period with large-scale settings of sacred texts and stories from the Bible – Mendelssohn's *Elijah*, for example, or Berlioz's *L'Enfance du Christ*, and huge settings of the Requiem by Verdi and Brahms.

Oratorios continue into the twentieth century with Elgar's *Dream of Gerontius*, Walton's *Belshazzar's Feast* and Britten's *War Requiem*. Such masterpieces are anything but remote. Every day (whether you're Christian or not) you can step into the great cathedrals and academic colleges of the UK and hear twentieth-century settings of the Eucharist in Te Deums and Masses. You can hear anthems, motets and choral compositions of every type. You can take part in the Evensong liturgy and hear (for free, remember) settings of the Magnificat, the Nunc dimittis and much more. What's more in King's College and St John's College, Cambridge and in New College and Magdalen College, Oxford, you'll hear them in some of the most breathtaking architectural locations in the world – for which in any other context you'd have to pay a fortune. And this is to leave out the scores of local parish churches that also have a strong choral tradition.

Throughout the twentieth century the beginnings of a more austere, pared-down and modern attitude towards religious music arrived in the form of Stravinsky's setting of the Mass for choir and wind instruments, of mystical organ music by Messiaen, or of Britten's settings of the Missa brevis. There are calm spiritual and meditative works by Arvo Paert and John Tavener – plus American composers such as Eric Whitacre and Morten Lauridsen, who are, incidentally, attracting a huge following on the Internet.

If, after all this lofty musical immersion, you long for something simpler you can step into any Christian church on a Sunday and join in with the hymns of Wesley and others and take part in congregational singing – the backbone of many traditional Anglican and Catholic services. Drop into the many thriving black Pentecostal churches if your taste is for something livelier. Here you'll experience vibrant and unrestrained melodies associated with gospel, soul and blues and sometimes wonder whether you really are in a church at all.

If you're a rock fan you'll be equally well-catered for in the Evangelical Christian Church. A couple of verses of 'Go Tell It on the Mountains' to the accompaniment of a guitar – or maybe two – have long since been replaced by electric guitars, keyboards and drums together with a burgeoning Christian music scene aimed specifically at the youth market. Try it out. It may be just what you've been waiting for. Or maybe it's not.

Halal or haram?

Many Muslims believe that music is a distraction from God and certainly over the years there has been unease in theological circles about the use of instruments (particularly stringed instruments) that come loaded with all sorts of secular and sensual connotations. It was instructive to note that when Cat Stevens, the triple-platinum-rated singer-songwriter converted to Islam in 1977, the first thing he did was to abandon the guitar and his singing career. It is equally interesting to note that, after presumably much thought and with a greater maturity underpinning his faith, he has decided to return to a performing career albeit with a repertoire of more reflective and devotional songs than of old.

But while more conservative Sunni and Shia scholars rule that music is incompatible with the faith, some of the mystical sects of Sufism incorporate music into their worship. While there is a perceptible difference in attitudes towards vocal and instrumental music, there is widespread agreement that performers and audience should be of the same sex.

But in western circles this is changing, too, with young people spearheading a minor musical revolution. If you're attracted to hip hop and rap, for example, then there is scope for developing your talent thanks to a newly emerging hip hop scene gathering momentum outside the mosque. Performances are mixed-sex affairs (though women performers invariably cover their hair and there is nothing of the secular 'club scene' about them). The rap is essentially vocal with sometimes drum and bass backbeat or a background techno drone.

Young Muslims are arguing that this style is very much in keeping with the recitation and the chanting of prayers, which is an uncontentious expression of the faith. Where performers have to work hard to persuade the scholars that their work is *halal* (permitted) or *haram* (forbidden) is in the lyrical content. Crudeness, violence, themes of misogyny, homophobia, promiscuity, crime and conspicuous material excess so prevalent in much secular rap are demonstrably absent from Muslim hip hop and are replaced by religious and socially aware themes performers would be happy to play to their mums and grans. Many still sport reverse baseball caps – a universal style signifier on which the imams have so far refrained from giving a religious ruling.

The real debate is whether music in and of itself is expressly forbidden in the Koran. Some scholars focus on verses such as those forbidding 'any vain or inglorious sound' and distinguish between sensual, earthly pursuits and right intentions that are directed towards worship and praise. Some also refer to the appearance of David in the Koran, to the Psalms being accompanied by a harp, and to angels singing and blowing trumpets round the throne of God. Sufism still carries the torch for Islamic sacred music but elsewhere the jury is still out. On balance, though, it would be fair to say that the conservative voices largely disapproving of music remain in the majority.

Baha'i and rastafarianism

For a musical tradition incorporating a reflective and meditative spirituality Baha'i worship offers many possibilities, though music plays an arguably less important role here than it does in other faiths. Services are simple but there are examples of homophonic 'hymns' for choirs and congregations. A large-scale choral music festival takes place annually showcasing the best of Baha'i singing and can display influences from such widely varying sources as gospel and Iranian folk singing.

At the other end of the musical spectrum, Rastafarianism offers a lively percussion and dance-based music with a fusion of African drumming, spirituals and gospel music known as Nyabinghi. But over the last 40 or so years it is reggae that has become the music most associated with the Rastafarian faith. The music carries the message of solidarity and uplift, encouraging the oppressed to look hopefully to the future – in particular to the rightful restoration of black people to their homeland of Africa. The incomparable Bob Marley is still its best-known and most popular exponent. And, frankly, what's not to adore about that?

Levi Roots (b. 1958), Rastafarian entrepreneur

*Rastafarianism is a **way of life**. It gives you something to hold on to beyond your own personal way of solving problems. When I was in the Dragons' Den, for instance, I believed there was **another power** helping me. Rastafarianism is very close to the Bible and **food and music** are spoken about often in the Bible. They go together.*

★★★
★★★

TOP THREE

1 At the risk of displaying a shamelessly western cultural bias, the top slot has undoubtedly to go to **Christianity** for music; its ability to tap into the sublime and to surprise with its variety and invention has to sit at the pinnacle of human achievement. From the simplest hymns and Psalms to the most intricate settings of the Passion narrative, other biblical texts and the Mass, the depth and richness of the music are unparalleled. Culturally biased? Well, not necessarily because remember that the works of Palestrina, Monteverdi, Bach, Mozart, Haydn, Beethoven, Mendelssohn, Verdi, Brahms, Stravinsky, Britten, Tavener and so on are performed throughout the world by people of all faiths and none, who can derive spiritual pleasure and comfort from works with a religious foundation without having to be card-carrying believers.

Remember also that your opportunities to hear world-class Christian religious music (often for free) are unrivalled. From university college chapels to the great cathedrals, Masses, motets, anthems, Psalms, settings of the Magnificat, the Nunc dimittis and other jewels of the liturgical repertoire are performed regularly by professional singers and instrumentalists, many of whom, incidentally, perform anonymously as sessions and backing musicians to luminaries of the pop and rock music world.

Get a Christian ticket (or perhaps borrow one) and you'll have access all areas.

2 **Hinduism** for the great ragas, Vedic chants, sitar and tabla instrumental music and for the incantatory, hypnotic and meditative state it can induce.

These days there are many opportunities to hear a variety of Hindu music – at the Womad Festival in the UK, for example, the Fez Sacred Music Festival in Morocco and the Chennai Music festival in southern India.

And, of course, there's always Bollywood if you're after something livelier, more popular, and, ahem, less spiritually demanding.

3 Islam for its haunting Sufi music comes close – but not close enough – to making the final three and in its place comes **Judaism** for the influence its practitioners have had on the course of the performing arts worldwide. Of the Academy Awards for Best Original Song, for example, over half have gone to Jewish composers; of those for Best Musical Scoring of a Film, just under half. Sixty-five per cent of those who have won a Tony for the Best Musical Production have been Jewish, rising to 72 per cent for those winning the category Best Original Score for a Musical. It's not strictly religious … oh all right, it's downright secular … but in some mysterious way music seems to be an essential this-worldly component of what *being* Jewish is all about.

So, you've got to hand it to them – from Rodgers and Hammerstein, to Stephen Sondheim, from George Gershwin to the *Fiddler on the Roof*.

04

Science

A golden age

Córdoba in Andalucia in southern Spain is, as every tourist knows, home to the breathtaking 'Great Mosque' (now a Christian cathedral) with its forest of columns supporting striped double arches the colour of honeycomb. Soaring heavenwards with a lightness that belies their architectural strength, surely these delicate barley-sugar sticks can't support the weight of this massive structure. But they do and have done for 11 centuries or thereabouts. It's a triumph of Islamic design and engineering, a fitting public building to grace what was once the most populous city in the world and the ancient capital of the Muslim caliphate of al-Andalus.

The Islamic imagination didn't stop there. Effortlessly juxtaposing the sublime with the mundane, the Arab town planners responsible for these sorts of things also introduced the world's first municipal rubbish bins, thereby ensuring that the surrounding streets would be fittingly spruce to showcase this and other masterpieces of Muslim civilization. The residents must have known this was a rather special place to live but what they could not have known was that they were living through what would later be called Islam's Golden Age, a time of unprecedented development in science, technology and philosophy throughout the Muslim world.

'The ink of the scholar is more holy than the blood of the martyr' was the guiding principle of the time (would it were still universally true today), as Islamic scientists and engineers pushed ahead in the fields of astronomy, physics, optics, chemistry and medicine. Mathematicians developed algebra and calculus and advanced our understanding of geometry and trigonometry, while physicians diagnosed measles and smallpox and developed surgical techniques that ensured the people of Córdoba, for example, had one of the highest life expectancy rates in the world.

If you're thinking of choosing Islam as a religion that can best express your commitment to science, you'll certainly be joining a tradition with a lengthy and honourable pedigree.

Fast-forward eleven hundred years, however, and such openness to the scientific method appeared, in one corner of London in 2011, to have been reversed if not forced into open retreat. For having dared to suggest that Darwin's theory of evolution is compatible with Islam, Dr Usama Hasan, a leading imam who also happened to be a university physics lecturer and fellow of the Royal Astronomical Society, was issued with death threats and dismissed from his position at the mosque. Dismissed, please note, not for saying the theory of evolution trumped Islam or invalidated it, but merely for saying that both positions could be held without any threat to either.

Of course the literalists who howled down Dr Hasan are not representative of mainstream Islamic scientific opinion but they highlight dramatically how even today some religious believers (in contrast perhaps to some of the more tolerant and enlightened populace of medieval Córdoba) feel science and religion are in conflict.

Galileo and Darwin

Christianity has similarly been suspicious of scientific enquiry at two key moments in its history. The first was in 1543 CE when the Roman Catholic Church, firm in its belief that the Earth, the pinnacle of God's Creation, was at the centre of the universe, had to confront a book suggesting that it might not be. The book had been written by the Polish astronomer Copernicus whose observations had led him to conclude that, on the contrary, the Earth might revolve around the Sun.

His hypothesis was taken up by the Italian astronomer Galileo Galilei whose own conclusions (that the Earth did indeed revolve around the Sun) threatened the Church's certainties and appeared to cast doubt on the omnipotence of a creator God. This was heresy.

Of course this hypothesis (soon to be proved as fact) did not question God's omnipotence at all, merely the Church's flawed and unscientific understanding of how God might have ordered Creation. The Church's view of the world had little to do with science and more to do with dogma, not to say pig-headedness. Still, the ecclesiastical authorities insisted they were right and that Galileo was wrong. All Galileo could counter his accusers with was observation, reason and the scientific method while they had recourse to hot pliers, branding irons and the rack. Galileo recanted.

Three hundred and fifty years later the naturalist Charles Darwin published his book *On the Origin of Species*, which outraged many within the Christian Establishment for suggesting the Genesis account of a fully created 'first man' in the form of Adam was a myth. Humankind had, Darwin maintained, evolved over millions of years from lower life forms by a process of natural selection. The fallout from this controversy continues to this day with creationists adamantly (appropriately enough) opposed to evolutionary biologists (some of them Christian and Muslim, incidentally), who beg to differ.

There are broadly four conclusions to be reached from these theological and scientific controversies. The first is that the two disciplines are in conflict and that science and religion are simply incompatible. The second is that each is independent of the other, neither in conflict nor in harmony, and constitute separate fields of enquiry. The third is that dialogue between the two is possible and that each can learn from the other's insights into phenomena that are common to both. And the fourth is that the two can be integrated into a single unified perspective. It's up to you to choose.

If you're considering choosing a religion you'll have no shortage of fundamentalisms to choose from. All the faiths number within them those who accept only a one-dimensional, literal and static interpretation of the text. They believe only what 'the Bible says' or what 'the Koran says' or what 'the Book of Mormon says' without even realizing that the words on the page are mute and need human interpretation.

On the other hand, you'll have at your disposal plenty of other faiths, sects and denominations that have no difficulty accepting simultaneously the claims of science and those of faith. In short, there are and have been many scientists who are religious – among them Copernicus, Galileo and Dr Hasan.

Faith in the scientific age

The Galilean and Darwinian blips aside, the Judaeo-Christian world view has largely coexisted fruitfully with scientific understanding – and for good reason. It teaches that matter, because it was created by God, is not to be feared or shunned, that there is order in the universe, and that there is unity in Creation. One God oversees and underpins this entity as opposed to many different gods controlling aspects of it. It can, therefore, be observed, recorded, weighed, measured and analysed in good conscience and to the glory of God.

Consequently that tradition has provided a background against which Jewish and Christian men and women of science from Hildegard of Bingen to Isaac Newton and Michael Faraday, from Albert Einstein to Robert Oppenheimer to Carl Sagan, have been able to share their insights in the pursuit of a better understanding of the material world.

With the Galileo issue firmly behind it, for instance, the Vatican actively promotes astronomical research. Not only does it have its own observatory in the grounds of the Pope's summer residence outside Rome but it sponsors independent scientific enquiry at its state-of-the-art observatory in Tucson, Arizona under the guidance of trained cosmologists many of whom are Jesuit priests. The unwritten maxim of their work could well be contained in the words of Isaac Newton: 'A little knowledge moves away from God, much knowledge leads towards Him.'

Islamic science is born out of the same theological tradition. The principle of unity (*tawhid*) implies that all that is, is of God and can therefore be studied. Indeed the Koran suggests there is a sacred duty to do so, as understanding the mysteries and beauty of the natural world can only enhance humanity's appreciation of the divine.

Perhaps the primal impetus for scientific enquiry has been the sky and all things visible and invisible therein. From the earliest times humans have scanned the heavens for some idea of their place within the immensity of the cosmos. Prehistoric monuments such as Stonehenge, Newgrange and the stone alignments of Karnak have acted, in some way, as celestial timepieces, allowing men and women to order both their spiritual and agricultural year.

It is not surprising, then, that astronomy has been a common theme of scientific enquiry down the ages. It is said, for instance, that the Three Wise Men who followed the bright star to Bethlehem and attended the birth of Jesus Christ were Zoroastrian astronomers from the East. The Copernican revolution and the idea of a Sun-centred solar system is also believed by many historians nowadays to owe much to the work of the Muslim astronomer Ibn al-Shatir over a century earlier. Noting the shortcomings of the earlier Ptolemaic model of an Earth-centred system he wrote, 'I therefore asked Almighty God to give me inspiration and help me invent models ... for the planetary motions ... free – thank God – from the doubts surrounding previous models.'

Astronomical theory had practical applications and spin-offs. Muslim astronomers made strides in optics and ground their own lenses. They invented astronomical instruments such as the quadrant and the astrolabe, which could also be used for calculating the direction of Mecca for the daily prayers. Thus the scientific fed into the technological, which then fed into the spiritual, which in turn served the scientific in one holistic and divinely ordered circularity. But there was far more to Islamic science than this.

In the five hundred years of its Golden Age, Islam powered developments in civil engineering, agriculture, medicine, chemistry, surgery, navigation, cryptography, surveying and disciplines and trades too numerous to mention. Their dams, wind- and watermills took water management to new levels of sophistication; their research into blood circulation and their pioneering surgical procedures saved the lives of many and prolonged the lives of many more. Their advances in textiles, paper and pottery were the envy of the world. The mathematicians of al-Andalus exported to Europe 'Arabic' numerals to replace Roman numerals, and their use of the decimal point, algebra and algorithms laid the foundations of computer technology today.

There was also space for life's luxuries from which we in the west benefited – and still do. Coffee was first imported into Britain by a Turkish merchant in the mid-seventeenth century CE, and in 1658 one of London's first coffee houses (The Sultan's Head) was opened in London, while in Brighton in 1759 the town's first Turkish baths appeared in the guise of the splendidly titled 'Mahomed's Indian Vapour Baths'.

With our westernized mindset and our Judaeo-Christian cultural heritage it is perhaps not surprising that what we refer to as Europe's 'Dark Ages' correspond quite neatly with Islam's 'Golden' ones, which only now are being given the prominence and acclaim they deserve. A rediscovery of the Islamic scientific legacy is long overdue.

So if you are considering Islam as a suitable religion within which to practise and further your understanding of science, it would be wise to seek out the true heirs to this glorious tradition and give a wide berth to those ignoramuses in east London who (like the medieval Christian church in Galileo's time) are quite prepared to shout down one of their own for daring to suggest that religion and science *are* compatible.

The eastern traditions

It is common in these days of the so-called 'war on terror' to refer to the 'clash of civilizations' argument, the notion that the religious and philosophical systems of some civilizations are fundamentally at war with those of another. At times of high tension and in the aftermath of murderous outrages such as 9/11 or the Madrid train bombings of 2004 such conclusions are perhaps understandable but do not always stand up to close scrutiny – not least because the murderers in question do not represent civilization in any sense that most of us would comprehend it.

Scholars have argued that true civilizations learn from each other. After all a good idea is a good idea in any language or culture. A case in point is that of Arabic numerals, which are also (if not widely) known as Hindu–Arabic numerals – thereby giving a pretty big clue to the joint provenance of this mathematical system. It takes no *Mastermind* champion to deduce, therefore, that just as Christian Europe shared mathematical ideas with the Muslims of Córdoba, so the Muslims of Baghdad shared mathematical ideas with the Hindus of Kashi (modern-day Varanasi). True civilizations do not clash, they dance.

The ninth-century-CE Muslim mathematician al-Khwarizmi, generally credited as the inspiration behind algebra, had himself studied Sanskrit and wrote a book explaining the Hindu system of numeration, which itself contained the first references to what is today known as the decimal scale. Three centuries later it was translated into Latin and circulated throughout Europe. While the credit went largely to al-Khwarizmi, it was left to Albert Einstein to note that, 'We owe a lot to the Indians who taught us how to count – without which no worthwhile scientific discovery could have been made.'

As early as 800 CE the Hindu sage Bharadwaj is credited with sowing the seeds of modern (Ayurvedic) medicine, which was built on four hundred years later by physicians pioneering surgical techniques and developments in the field of gynaecology, anatomy and anaesthesia. Although it's disputed that the astronomer Aryabhatt posited the idea that the Earth revolves around the Sun – and did so some 1,000 years before Copernicus – his genius as a mathematician is not in doubt. It is he who is credited with calculating pi to four decimal places and, perhaps most significantly of all, with inventing the concept of zero.

All in all, then, from botany to geography, from metallurgy to chemistry (and all of the above), the Hindu tradition is a pretty rich one to consider.

It has been said that the Chinese traditions of Taoism, Confucianism and Buddhism have not been sympathetic to traditional science since the scientific method, being allegedly too concerned with the materiality of the universe, has failed to grasp the true nature of the world. But things are changing. Not least with Quantum Theory and Heisenberg's

Uncertainty Principle, which states that if you know where a particle is you don't know how fast it's moving and that if you do know how fast it's moving, you don't know where it is. No, please don't ask. Look it up for yourself because my brain is beginning to hurt.

Let's leave this one to Robert Oppenheimer who wrote in his book *Science and the Common Understanding*:

> If we ask, for instance, whether the position of the electron remains the same, we must say 'no'; if we ask whether the electron's position changes with time, we must say 'no'; if we ask whether the electron is at rest, we must say 'no'; if we ask whether it is in motion, we must say 'no'. The Buddha has given such answers when interrogated as to the conditions of man's self after his death.

And what about this clincher?

> There must be no barriers to freedom of enquiry. There is no place for dogma in science. The scientist is free, and must be free to ask any question, to doubt any assertion, to seek for any evidence, to correct any errors.

Well said, Bob.

TOP THREE ★★★★★

In strictly chronological order:

1 **Hinduism**
2 **Judaeo-Christianity**
3 **Islam**

05

Literature

People of the book

'What you have in hand,' wrote the scholar George Steiner in his masterly introduction to the Everyman edition of the Old Testament or Hebrew Bible, 'is not *a* book. It is *the* book... It is the book which, not only in western humanity, defines the concept of a text.'

As befits its importance, the Torah ('instructions' or 'guidance', and the core of Jewish law) is given pride of place in the synagogue. Comprising the first five books of the Hebrew Bible, it is hand-copied by scribes onto scrolls, wrapped in a mantle of embroidered brocade topped with silver finials, and housed in the Ark behind a curtain or door where symbolically and actually it presides over the worship. It is that important. Little wonder, then, that Christians call their scripture, the Old and New Testament combined, the *Holy* Bible or, with colloquial solemnity, the Good Book.

To Muslims the Koran enjoys the same sacred status. Not any book but *the* book, breathed into life by God, recited by the Prophet to his followers, transcribed into Holy Writ, and binding for all time on the faithful. It is customary to place it on the highest shelf, above all other texts, to show it respect and, for the same reason, not to turn one's back on it.

It's clear that for those within these different traditions the books are invested with a quality that elevates them above mere literature. That's why fundamentalist Christian pastors who see fit to burn Korans on one side of the world should expect fireworks on the other – and, to be honest, despite their protestations of surprise after the event, probably do (likewise, Muslims who burn flags or poppies, but that's perhaps a different story). The Koran is not only a text meshing the temporal lives of the faithful with the eternal plan of the Almighty, it is also a badge of identity and an emblem of belonging. What you do to it you might also start doing to its readers.

Not for nothing did the Nazis raid synagogues and desecrate Torah scrolls as a prelude to the Final Solution. They were helpfully sending out a signal that the world sadly either misread or ignored – despite a prescient remark by the nineteenth-century German poet Heinrich Heine who, Cassandra-like, remarked that 'where they have burned books, they will end up burning human beings'. To repeat: literature, books, words matter.

But let's lighten the mood for a moment and look at the content of these books. To have lasted so long (and, in the case of the Bible, to have been translated into over two thousand languages and to have shifted more copies than Harry Potter or the *Highway Code*) they must be a good read. They are – though not always an easy one.

One book, many books

If you're compiling a religious/literary checklist and totting up the scores on a 1-to-10 scale of highpoints, be prepared to rate the Hebrew Bible/Old Testament pretty highly. You might not always like what you read, and the content may confirm your worst suspicions about an angry, vengeful God who punishes and smites at the drop of a hat. That's at least partly because a lot of the text deals with an angry, vengeful God who punishes and smites at the drop of a hat. Though, of course, if that were all God did it would make for a pretty one-dimensional read. Ditto, if the plots hinged solely on punishments and smitings. The Old Testament can claim, with rather more veracity than the old *News of the World* boast, that indeed 'all human life is there'. With or without the exclamation mark.

It's history, it's poetry, it's family trees, it's law. It's prayers, songs, wisdom – and cracking good yarns capable of being endlessly retold. Indeed, one of the great things about these stories – and something they have in common with the most durable tales that have their origins in the oral tradition – is that you can embellish them in the telling and still retain the power. But such is their careful, house-of-cards-like structure (like the best Jewish jokes) that you can add to them in moderation – but never take away.

You can retell the story of Adam and Eve and add supplementary detail about flora and fauna, building it up to a big finish and milking the drama for all it's worth with asides about motivation, and nakedness, and lack of shame. But leave out the snake and you've got no story. Likewise, you can add any number of animals to Noah's Ark, rounding up aardvarks and axolotls, zebras and zorillas until you're sounding like David Attenborough on a roll. But forget to mention that they go in two by two and you break the rhythm. Forget to mention the dove and the rainbow at the end and, if you're retelling the story to kids, you'll have a mutiny on your hands because the story doesn't work without them.

But, to continue. Pretty soon after the Garden of Eden we're into the pivotal Jewish narrative of Abraham (né Abram), his Covenant with the Lord, and the long journey of his people towards the Promised Land (to be continued in subsequent episodes). It's the screenplay for a road movie. Along the way, after two incidents of wife-swapping and a tragically illegitimate child whom Abraham feels impelled to banish from the tribe (is this a mere 'story', by the way, or the root of the Arab–Israeli conflict today?), his wife bears him a son, Isaac. And then, in one of the most baffling and poignant narratives in the entire Bible (one that has provoked psychological and philosophical interpretations by luminaries as diverse as Kierkegaard and Leonard Cohen), Abraham prepares to kill this longed-for child and sacrifice him to the Lord – only to be spared the task at the last minute. *EastEnders* and *Coronation Street* couldn't come up with better plot lines, characters or cliff-hangers.

There are stories of a similar order too numerous to mention: plagues of Egypt, walls of Jericho, valleys of bones and dens of lions. There are stories of strength, resolve and courage (Samson and Delilah, David and Goliath); there are stories of tenderness and devotion (Ruth and Naomi), and stories reflecting every aspect of the human condition.

And alongside the stories, of course, is the poetry of which the 150 Psalms are perhaps the best-known examples. Expressing the highs and lows of the human experience these songs of praise and lamentation, of sorrow and yearning, of joy, doubt, worship, trust and faithfulness express not only the full range of Israel's faith and experience but arguably encapsulate the existential concerns of anyone wrestling with the complexities of faith.

A new testament

If you're looking to Christianity as a source of literary satisfaction, you can include all above in the mix – but with reservations. Christians generally read the Old Testament in the light of the New and see in it pointers towards a new order of which Jesus Christ is the fulfilment. Which, of course, is not how you'd read it if you were thinking of becoming a Jew.

In some ways the majesty and brilliance of the King James Version of the Bible have contributed to this unfortunate misapprehension. The very genius of the translation has lent the text all the characteristics of an English (and, by inference, Christian) classic. Moreover, uniformity of language and style suggest a seamless transition between a society living in expectation of a Messiah and a society into which (whether people accepted it or not) the Messiah had stepped. For those who would come to call themselves Christians this might be true but for Jews who remained within their own faith it would not be.

However. if you're thinking of picking Christianity on literary merit, you'll be looking at an altogether different narrative structure in the New Testament. The first three Gospels (literally 'good news') contain accounts of the life and ministry of Jesus of Nazareth as seen from similar points of view, sharing some material but each introducing elements of the author's own. They're titled gospels *according* to Matthew, Mark and Luke, suggesting that they are not three different stories but rather three accounts of the same basic story.

Crucially they contain details of Jesus' death and resurrection. The Fourth Gospel according to John is quite different in tone and does not have the same sense of reportage and immediacy. Rather it's more like an analysis of or reflection on the significance of the events described.

The picture that emerges is of a charismatic healer, teacher and preacher whose radical message of salvation upsets the religious status quo of first-century Palestine and prompts a sacrificial death on the cross. The four gospels are not biographical in the conventional sense. They have a real historical basis but, according to the conventions of the day, include material that has been gathered from a number of oral sources and assembled to support a particular aspect of Jesus' character the writer thought important.

This is particularly true of the birth narratives that are contained only in Mathew and Luke and vary in some of the detail. Whether this is an historical portrayal of the events surrounding Christ's Nativity is the subject of some theological debate. There are those who claim that the very fact that there is discrepancy is proof that jointly the writers are reporting facts as reported to them. Total unanimity on times, places, dates, details might have suggested the two were in cahoots and more in the propaganda business than concerned about the objective recording of these strange and powerful events. What people reading the text through the eyes of faith conclude, however, is that there is a greater underlying truth being described that is all the more persuasive for having been set down discrepancies and all.

The force of the gospels comes from the blend of strength and gentleness present in the person of Jesus himself. His parables and sermons are masterpieces of concision and storytelling with layers of complexity belying the superficially simple style. But it is perhaps in the accounts of Jesus' final days on Earth that the narratives achieve both greater unanimity and an emotional power arguably unsurpassed in sacred literature.

The Passion narrative is poignant in the way it portrays the disciples in all their flawed humanity – one moment

professing their faithfulness, the next moment fearfully
denying their discipleship to avoid punishment themselves.
In these portrayals we see ourselves and it is the combination
of psychological truth and drama that lends these stories
their power.

After this there is the equally dramatic account of the
Resurrection, then the Descent of the Holy Spirit on the
disciples and the start of the worldwide Christian mission. For
anyone considering taking up the Christian way there could
be no better way of describing the shared sense of excitement
at the task ahead.

The Koran

Would-be Muslims have an entirely different literary style
to confront. The Koran consists of 114 surahs, or chapters,
varying in length from three to over 250 verses. Since the
revelation came to the Prophet bit by bit over a period of
23 years, material was inserted in different sections and not
always in chronological order.

To readers more used to a linear flow of narrative the
Koranic texts do not make for easy reading. There are
frequent repetitions, for example, but these are deliberate
as the book exists not just to tell stories but to instruct the
faithful in every aspect of God's law.

Reinforcing God's message and encouraging the faithful to
take the right path are part of the book's main spiritual and
educational purpose. Stylistically it makes more sense once
the person coming to it realizes that it is not meant to be a
book read in one sitting. Portions of it may be read out as part
of worship – or even as part of prayers – and the non-linear
aspect to it, darting back and forth to address this or that
aspect of Muslim practice and law, makes the chosen portion
a self-contained lesson in itself. The overwhelming tone is
didactic rather than descriptive but it doesn't stop countless
young people wanting to learn the whole thing by heart.
Certainly when recited in the original Arabic, the language of
God, the effect is both powerful and beautiful even if one has
no Arabic at all.

Action and excitement

The Hindu sacred texts embrace a variety of styles. The earliest take the form of the Vedas, Sanskrit collections of hymns from the oral tradition. The Rig Veda is the earliest of them all, dating from around 1200 BCE. It has to be said that this and later collections with their spells and ritual instructions aren't exactly an easy read for the newcomer to the faith.

It is with the *Mahabharata*, one of Hinduism's two major Sanskrit epics, that something like a western narrative emerges. However, containing some 200,000 lines and reckoned to be the largest single poem in the world, it's not something you're going to knock off on the bus home. The epic is the story of the war between the five Pandava brothers, helped by their distant relative, Krishna, and their 100 cousins. It's a tale revolving round the question of who is to be the rightful ruler of the land and gains sophisticated emotional force from the different approaches the brothers bring to the realities of fighting.

The central section is perhaps the best known, the Bhagavad Gita, or 'Song of the Lord'. Essentially it is a conversation between one of the brothers, Arjuna, and his charioteer (who, it transpires, is Lord Krishna himself). Although overtly about the imminent battle, the conversation is an allegory of the soul's striving for spiritual liberation and is, in parts, very moving. The other great Hindu epic is the *Ramayana*, which is about a quarter of the size of the *Mahabharata* and tells of the adventures of Prince Rama whose wife Sita has been abducted by Ravana, the demon king of Lanka. The story is used to explore the themes of morality and right behaviour in society and contains both philosophical and devotional elements.

Guides for living

In Sikhism the scriptures, the Adi Granth (the First Book), are accorded the highest respect – so much so that they are treated as a living guru and known as the Guru Granth Sahib. As the presiding official reads from the text, he or she waves a small whisk over the pages in commemoration of the way in which historically royalty and visiting dignitaries were fanned to keep them cool.

They contain the writings of the gurus, prayers to be recited both at home and in the gurdwara, and devotional hymns. These scriptures, central to Sikh faith and identity, are reflections on the nature and truth of God.

Like the Sikh hymns, Buddhist sacred texts are not literature in the way we in the west would understand it. The best known of these is probably the Chinese Diamond Sutra, which, dated around 868 CE, is the oldest printed book in existence and contains the texts of sermons preached by the Buddha.

The *Tao Te Ching*, or 'Classic of the Way and Its Power', is the central text of Taoism and is said to have been written by the sage Lao Tzu around the sixth century CE. Among other things it teaches that by harmonizing the complementary forces of yin and yang spiritual (and physical) health will ensue.

These eastern texts often seem impenetrable at first sight and are far removed from the pictorial, dramatic and essentially linear narrative techniques of western scripture. Very often they derive their power from being chanted, often in groups.

1 **Judaism** for the Book of books, the incomparable Hebrew Bible. Also for the fruitful rebelliousness it's given rise to in non-religious writers. Like Saul Bellow, who, though insisting he was not a Jewish writer per se, illuminates a kind of alienation that seems to be part of the Jewish experience; like Philip Roth, who wants to break free of Judaism but also hankers after its attachments; and like the more overtly religious Isaac Bashevis Singer, who argues with God, is hurt by God, but remains faithful nonetheless.

2 **Christianity** for the themes of love and self-sacrifice suffering and redemption explored by writers such as Tolstoy and Dostoyevsky. And also for the great spiritual classics that take the biblical themes and rework them: the *Divine Comedy*, *Paradise Lost*, *The Pilgrim's Progress*.

3 **Hindusim** for the Bhagavad Gita and its disquisition on the spiritual battle the soul needs to fight until it comes to God.

06

Family

Home is where the faith is

Open the pages of any book on world religions and you will be struck by the number of times children feature in the pictures and illustrations. And there is good reason for this. Religion *begins* in the family. It is from the parent or parents or those *in loco parentis* that children first get their view of the world, the universe and their place within both. Though nature will take its course (why else would people convert from one religion to another?), parental nurture will exert a pull many children feel neither able nor willing to resist for many, many years. We are all Freudians now. Even though many religious people might at first struggle to deny it.

It is in the home that children learn, for good or ill, their foundational values, values like their relationship to power and authority and to those weaker than themselves. It is in the home crucially that they learn the meaning of selflessness, cooperation, kindness, interdependence and unconditional love. Some, of course, through cruelty or neglect, learn the reverse of these universal values and waste years in adult life wondering why the world is generally against them. But that is another story.

Judaism was arguably the first religion to realize that the survival of the faith (and, by extension, the survival of the Jewish people) depends on the family. Don't imagine, though, if you're considering the Jewish option, that you'll automatically be walking into the 1950s chocolate-box world of the untroubled nuclear family complete with two smiling parents and two well-scrubbed children roasting chestnuts by an open fire. As Tolstoy could have said (but inexplicably chose not to): 'All happy families are the same. Jewish families are different.' Not, one hastens to add, that they are unhappy. It's just that the concept of happiness per se is not a primary driver. Obeying God comes first and happiness will flow from it. That, at least, is the theory – though even the rabbis have spotted the flaw in that one.

Remember that 'Israel' (which became Jacob's given name after he had spent all night wrestling with the angel) means 'one who argues with God'. So expect noise and disputation, arguments and disagreement alongside the conventional picture of domestic harmony. If the family has ensured the survival of the faith, it is often said that the Sabbath has supported the family for it is in the home that the rituals of the faith are performed.

On Friday night as the Shabbat (Sabbath) is ushered in over a shared meal the table becomes an altar and the parents the temple priests of old, sanctifying the bread and wine, and thanking God for the gift of Creation. As the mother lights two Shabbat candles and says the blessing ('Blessed art thou, King of the Universe, who hast hallowed us by the commandments') this simple homely scene becomes nothing less than the intersection of the domestic and the cosmic – and an otherwise unremarkable family from Golders Green or Gateshead can sit down to supper bathed in the spirit of the Almighty.

The celebratory Seder meal eaten on the first night of Passover in remembrance of the Exodus from Egypt is also such a moment. As the youngest family member asks aloud, 'Why is this night different from all other nights?' what looks like a boisterous family get-together is transformed into an event in and out of time, adding another unseen link to the 3,500-year-old chain of Jewish history. Compared to this sort of thing non-Jewish family occasions could be said to be a bit on the bland side. But other religious traditions have their riches, too.

Rights and responsibilities

Family life was much praised by the Buddha, who compared its members to the trees in a forest, which jointly can withstand the force of the wind while a single tree, however tall and strong, cannot. Consequently Buddhist families (in common, to be fair, with all truly religious families) are interdependent units where parents and children are assigned rights but where mutual responsibilities are expected in return.

Consequently, children are expected to honour and support their parents and maintain the family traditions while parents are to restrain their children from evil, attend to their education, see that they are married at a proper age, and hand over to them their inheritance in due course. Play this particular game by the right rules, then, and you shouldn't find yourself cut out of Dad's will when the time comes to collect.

Similarly, the ground rules are laid down in advance for the husband and wife. The husband should be courteous, respectful and faithful (no surprises there) but also, according to the book of Buddhist ethics known as the Digha Nikaya, provide her with clothes and adornments (which for the fashion-conscious wife is an unexpected religious bonus). In return, the wife should be faithful (*natch*), perform her household duties well, be hospitable to relatives, and protect the family income. Though this last condition does seem a rather shrewd rider to the 'clothes and adornment' clause, it doesn't invalidate the mutual obligations shown by one to the other. The obligations are all the more touching for being written down in black and white, as it were, as part of an extensive code of generally accepted family behaviour.

Should you be attracted to Confucianism, the ethical/philosophical system developed in the fifth century BCE by the Chinese sage K'ung-fu-tzu (Confucius; currently enjoying a revival in China after falling out of favour under Chairman Mao), you will be expected to view your obligations within the family circle with the utmost seriousness. One of the core principles of Confucianism is 'filial piety', a concept whereby children (and sons in particular) are expected not only to show honour to their parents but also to make sacrifices for them and avoid bringing the family name into disrepute. They should show them courtesy at all times and ensure that they study well in order to get a good job that will provide the material means of supporting them in old age. Filial duties don't stop with the death of the parents either, because children are expected to be diligent in their performance of elaborate rituals at the graves of the ancestors.

All in all, Confucianism is not a world view to be recommended to people who are naturally rebellious by nature. It expects conformity and order (not for nothing were Confucian scriptures required reading for those taking the entrance examinations for the imperial civil service). Implicit in the concept of filial piety is not only respect between father and son but also between ruler and ruled, between friend and friend, and, by extension, between company and employees, thereby ensuring in principle the smooth running of society at all levels. If you are one of those people temperamentally inclined to go against the grain of things (and to stand up and complain if you judge the supposed smooth running of society not to be quite so smooth as you would like) then Confucianism is probably not for you.

Extended families

I couldn't be sure but I feel pretty confident in asserting that any aspiring Hindu stand-up comedian relying on mother-in-law gags to tickle an audience had better hang on to his day job.

On the Indian subcontinent up until the middle of the twentieth century it was commonplace to see three or four generations of a family living together under one roof. This communal life relied on all working members pooling their income to support each other. Tasks were allotted according to an accepted hierarchy. Women ruled over the kitchen preparing food for the household, for example, while the older men decided how the finances were to be organized. Education for the youngsters had to be paid for, marriage expenses had to be budgeted for and, in rural areas, farming tools had to be bought. The entire household, therefore, operated on communal lines with older, wiser and (usually but not solely) male heads presiding over its everyday running. And, just as 'Eskimos' were once said (wrongly, as it turns out) to have a dozen words for 'snow', Hindus have more than one word to describe relationships with their relatives. In Britain an aunt is an aunt is an aunt whereas in Hindi, Gujarati or Punjabi different words are used to describe your mother's sister, your father's sister, your mother's brother's wife, or your father's brother's wife.

Traditional Sikh families also observe the unwritten conventions of extended or joint family life. From very early on in his or her life a child is familiar with what to outsiders are the baffling intricacies of shared intergenerational living. Young girls and boys, for example, appreciate instinctively the limits of playfulness and the boundaries of respect. They know how far they can go in teasing their older relatives; playing tricks on their sister's husband's younger brother, for example, is acceptable while practising similar japes with his older brother (if he has one) is not.

As a result of increasing urbanization the pattern of shared housing is fragmenting even in India but in the industrialized west it has always had to compromise – if only because most houses and flats are too small to accommodate the numbers. But the relationships still apply and, unless you're a hardcore family enthusiast at heart, the Hindu or Sikh arrangement is not going to be for you. If you're the type that likes to come home to a quiet oasis, retreat to your shed or sewing room and spend an evening on your own in peace and quiet, family life in a Hindu home would most probably drive you nuts. If, on the contrary, you relish the intergenerational communality of a shared household, you will love it. And you can be confident that, however old and frail you become, you will never be a burden and you will never be alone.

Those wanting a glimpse into the ups and downs of such a family arrangement could do worse than watch Mira Nair's 2002 film classic *Monsoon Wedding* set in modern day Delhi in the Verma household on the eve of their daughter's wedding. As the entire clan arrives from home and abroad the frustrations, the tensions and the joys of this interwoven tapestry of extended family life are portrayed in loving though not uncritical detail. Comic, tragic and romantic by turns the film is also realistic in its honest depiction of how members of an essentially ordinary religious family must inevitably make compromises under the manifold pressures of everyday non-religious life. You're drawn to the eastern religious family life? Here's a taste of what it might entail.

Happy families?

A close family is all very well ('all happy families are the same', remember), but what are you to do if for one reason or another you want to leave it and strike out on your own? The religions deal with this eventuality in different ways and you'd be well advised to study their record before signing up to any faith or denomination.

Most families hope and expect that you will stay. Consequently, leaving the family (especially leaving a village for the bright lights of the city) causes disappointment and sadness. But in many cultures your departure might also cause shame, for which punishment is sometimes demanded. It may amount to a personal rebuke, or perhaps to complete ostracism and disinheritance or, as we have seen earlier with the young woman grievously abused by the Taliban, to something much worse.

However, when leaving the family also involves *leaving the faith* the consequences (for what in some communities is seen as a form of betrayal) can be dire. Threats of intimidation, violence and even murder for the 'crime' of apostasy (renunciation of belief in a particular religion) are not uncommon and have been made most vociferously of late by some extremists within the Muslim community. Though not widespread in the west, such threats have been made and carried out in other parts of the world.

Similarly punishments and even so-called 'honour killings' have been carried out on those deemed to have brought shame on a family, either by resisting an arranged marriage or by flouting parental authority and choosing to marry outside their religion or social class. Some within the Muslim, Hindu and Sikh communities have been accused of turning a blind eye to such incidents (on the rare occasions that they occur) and are being encouraged to condemn them unequivocally. Scholars from all faiths have stepped in to calm things down by pointing out that the religious texts themselves forbid such abuses, which are essentially cultural and historical in origin and indefensible in religious terms.

With the breakdown of traditional family structures in the west it is easy to underestimate the psychological pain felt by a family when members leave and appear to affiliate themselves to an alien creed or culture. The roots of the tension go deep and usually originate at a time when and in a place where the act of leaving (it would have been considered nothing short of desertion at the time) threatened the survival of the group and warranted exemplary punishment as a consequence. Minority religious communities living within the increasingly secularized west feel this threat most keenly today and feel that the boy who takes to drinking and smoking or the girl who abandons traditional dress for western fashion is somehow jeopardizing the very survival of the tribe.

Various Christian and Jewish minorities in this country have had longer to adjust to the pressures of a prevailing culture and have learned to make concessions to the mainstream. Even so, you only have to look to some smaller Christian sects who have completely isolated themselves from secular society to see how they deal with rebellion in their midst. The Amish in the USA, for example, react sharply to those rejecting communal norms of behaviour and punish it with outright rejection. Those who have transgressed are 'shunned' or 'disfellowshipped' and effectively banished into outer darkness by people who earlier had been their friends and co-religionists. There is, however, a built-in safety valve – the so-called *rumspringa* when adolescents are permitted to go a little wild. You could call it a gap year in rebelliousness and the sowing of wild oats after which they decide whether the Amish communal life is for them. Perhaps surprisingly, for most it is and they willingly return to follow the family patterns of their parents and grandparents. Once this carefree period is over, however, conformity is expected and required. Remaining within the fold is part of the deal.

Some Jewish families, too, often view 'marrying out' as not only a slap in the face to the family but (albeit subconsciously) as an act of betrayal to the community – although in a pluralistic society such as Britain non-Orthodox Jews in particular take a more accommodating view of the phenomenon. They accept the reality of mixed marriages and, rather than censuring the Jewish partner (thereby driving them away), will do everything to make both parties welcome at the synagogue.

A characteristically good-humoured story from the celebrated and self-confessed gay rabbi Lionel Blue throws light on some of the other tensions within the Jewish family, revealing how difficult it often is for the parents to let go.

Lionel was born in the East End of London to parents who had arrived from eastern Europe as penniless refugees. They had worked hard and vested all their love in young Lionel who, as an obviously bright boy, was destined for greater things. He excelled in his studies and, to his parents' delight, went on to Oxford where a glittering future beckoned. Yes, his mother reasoned, Lionel will go far in the world, he will move out of the East End poverty he has known and in due course make enough money to take us with him.

But this was not to be for Lionel had other plans. No, he didn't want to move away; on the contrary he wanted to return to his East End roots and be a rabbi to the Jewish community there. For the time being, however, he kept this to himself for he had a bigger secret that was weighing him down. He had come to realize he was homosexual and, in a community where this was viewed as sinful, wondered how he would be able to break the news to his family. In time he explained all to his parents who took the admission with understanding and equanimity. Then came the other piece of news that, after all the education he had received at Oxford, he intended to settle not in the leafy suburbs of Golders Green but back in the inner-city ghetto of the East End.

This time his mother's reaction was quite different. Inconsolable, she wailed, 'How can you do this, Lionel? To come back here after all the opportunities we've given you!' Then she added, neatly turning his earlier confession in her favour, 'Thank goodness you're never going to have any children of your own. At least you'll be spared the pain they can inflict on their poor parents.' This last observation was not a generalized complaint but one deliberately targeted. Lionel, of course, was an only child.

Rabbi Lionel Blue (b. 1930), writer and broadcaster

*I'm a Jew because I was born a Jew but I remain a Jew for many reasons. For one it answers many **practical** needs at the moment. I'm a gay person, I live with my partner and Judaism is very good at enabling you to **make family out of friends**, which is a wonderful thing as loneliness is one of the great dangers in life, particularly in places like London. We keep the Jewish Sabbath and invite friends round (Jewish and non-Jewish) to share the Friday night meal and there's a kind of magic in it. I'm always touched when a hush descends and the candles are lit. You've got everything on the kitchen table that you'd see on an altar in a Christian church; bread wine, candlesticks but they'll all be beside the mustard pot and the tomato sauce. I love the **domestic** feel of it all.*

*When I speak to God I don't think in terms of family relationships. I don't think of God as father or mother or that sort of thing because I don't want to project onto the cosmos the Blue's family problems. **I chat to God all the time** and sometimes we just sit in silence together.*

*It used to be difficult being gay and Jewish but less so now. If you're delving into the Bible you're dealing with the mores of a Semitic world in its late Bronze Age and I don't think all the things that applied then apply now. I mean slavery's gone, polygamy's gone, having concubines has gone, castration of your foe has gone, all sorts of nasty ways of death have gone. **Thank God things change.** The place of women in society has changed and the status of gay people has changed. And it's about time, too.*

*There are pluses and minuses in Jewish family life. First of all it's very warm but sometimes the love comes with strings attached. You have uncles, aunts, cousins and people who appeared from nowhere and got absorbed into your family. And there's always been a tradition of **hospitality** in Jewish life. Food is very important in Jewish life. In western religion God usually comes to you through your mind. In Judaism it often comes through the taste buds. If you took me into* *a Jewish kitchen I could sniff around and tell what festival we're coming up to. Each festival has its different kinds of food and it means there's a perpetual party you're waiting for.*

*One of the great characteristics of Jewish spirituality is that you do it through **argument** and sometimes this can get out of hand. They always say, 'Any Jewish congregation which doesn't try to get rid of its rabbi isn't truly Jewish. And any rabbi who allows them to get away with it isn't a real rabbi.'*

Priestly families

If you're attracted to family life in devout religious households it's as well to bear in mind an extra expectation that some of them may harbour on your behalf; namely, that you renounce the very family life you're enjoying in order to become a priest, a monk or a nun. Realistically, however (and not to be ageist about this), the likelihood is that, if you've bought this book with your own money, this option will not apply. But it's all useful information to arm yourself with and you may want to pass it on.

Although the latest figures show an alarming decline in Catholic vocations, it has long been the desire of devout Catholics to see at least one of their sons going on to the seminary to study for the priesthood. Some others (though probably rather fewer) actively wish their sons and daughters to take up the contemplative life completely and become monks and nuns. With the exception of those married Anglican priests who have joined the Catholic Church, the celibate life is a requirement for those training for the priesthood or entering the monastery or convent. Although there is a small movement within the Church for change it is unlikely that this requirement will be dropped in anything like the near future – if ever.

While the Buddha encouraged family life he also set great store by the monastic tradition, which generally, though in some Korean, Tibetan and Japanese schools not exclusively, requires celibacy. So, if you're led towards greater devotional practices in the Buddhist tradition you can, if you choose carefully, have your cake and eat it.

Sikhism, by contrast, has no monastic or ascetic tradition. All the gurus were married men and Guru Nanak, the founder of Sikhism, said that contemplation of the divine name is quite possible within the hurly-burly of life and added, with arguably just a touch of condescension, 'Such is the greatness of the True guru that through divine grace and guidance one can attain liberation even while surrounded by sons and wife.'

But it's probably Judaism that most actively and unequivocally promotes family life as a positive religious virtue. Not only are celibacy and asceticism entirely alien to Jewish practice, there is also a tradition stating that on the Day of Judgement Jews will be asked to account not only for their sins but also for the legitimate pleasures they denied themselves in life. A nice touch that and one guaranteeing the pleasures of the marital bed to would-be adherents.

Hinduism has an interesting take on asceticism and, in theory at least, weaves it into the very fabric of family life. Traditionally there are four ashramas, or stages in life, that a man is expected to pass through on the long journey towards spiritual liberation. The first is that of the student immersing himself in study of the religious texts; the second is that of the householder providing for his wife and extended family; the third is retirement from active work and retreat into meditation and reading; and the fourth is withdrawal from all worldly attachments including wife, family and home to devote the remainder of his present life to spiritual matters alone. Not everyone follows this last stage these days but the mere fact that it is still in the rulebook emphasizes that even family life has a fixed duration in the scheme of things and, in the final analysis, is secondary to the life of the spirit.

1 Although all the world religions cherish family life it is perhaps **Judaism** that accords it the highest place, seeing it as both a religious duty and as a temporal joy. No families are perfect and Jewish families – fractious and argumentative, accepting and disapproving, loving and judgemental by turns – are no different. But they are arguably unique in placing the family as an institution at the centre of their worshipping lives. It all began with Abraham, whom God promised to make the father of a great nation, and it's been going on for three and a half thousand years. Not a bad record on the whole.

2 The **Hindu** and **Sikh** concept of the extended family where all the generations live under the same roof with a sophisticated hierarchical structure ruling their conduct towards each other may not be to everybody's taste. In a world influenced by the *Grand Designs* school of living where everybody has his or her own 'personal space', this mass sharing of communal premises may seem intolerably intrusive. But for its interdependence, its respect and care for the strong and the weak alike, and for the utter redundancy of the words 'lonely' and 'neglected', it's surely hard to beat. Just a shame that housing in the west isn't geared to more of it.

3 On the face of it the Jesus we read about in the New Testament has a dismissive view of family life. He can be very brusque with his mother at times and whatever she and his rather peripheral stepfather have to say does not dissuade him from leaving the family business and getting on with his own job of salvation and redeeming the world from sin. But in practice, and at their best, **Christian** families are loving and supportive. Of course, some denominations can be restrictive to the point of suffocation but across the great spread of the Christian traditions there is a great acceptance of childhood rebellion and a ready acceptance to welcome errant members back into the fold. The Parable of the Prodigal Son probably explains it all.

07

Sex

Body and spirit

When asked by a magazine reporter what she thought of sex, the screen goddess Marilyn Monroe is said to have replied, 'I think it's here to stay.' The great religious sages down the years have been inclined to agree with her though at least one (St Augustine) fervently wished it didn't have to be. We'll come to him in a moment since he's been largely (if unintentionally) responsible for stigmatizing sex and has a lot to answer for in having made countless generations of Christian men and women distinctly uneasy with and/or ashamed of this most primal of acts. It is, after all, the most fun you can have without laughing.

By and large the eastern religions have avoided this trap and have taken a holistic view of life as a synthesis of the mental, the physical and the spiritual. While Augustine saw the body as inimical to the spirit, eastern philosophers have seen it as a vibrant, necessary and hallowed part of life.

So, of the four goals of classical Hinduism, *kama* specifically enjoins sensual, physical and emotional pleasure (the others are *dharma*, righteousness, duty or virtue; *artha*, legitimate wealth and social status; and *moksha*, spiritual liberation from death and rebirth). In other words, if you're keen on sex with the lights on, sex al fresco, and sexual intercourse in more positions than the early western missionaries had envisaged, you'll find it in Hinduism because the texts have officially sanctioned it. Not that they have sanctioned licentiousness and promiscuity, however. Far from it. The texts and the sages have seen the sexual act as one of the supreme expressions of humankind's yearning for communion with the Ultimate and, as such, it is not to be sullied by mere philandering. And, by way of a bonus, Hinduism not only celebrates sexuality but, in some cases, helpfully provides manuals (the *Kama Sutra* and the *Koka Shastra*) for improving your technique.

To be fair to the Jewish tradition, it, too, has always recognized the physical element in life and continues to celebrate sexuality as one of the gifts of the Creator to be enjoyed in its proper place and at the proper time (more anon). It, too, has its biblical text to sanctify the joys of the sexual act, the Song of Solomon (aka the Song of Songs), which is an unmistakably erotic poem on the bliss of physical union between a man and a woman.

Although taken to be an allegory of the love between God and Israel or God and Creation or God and the Church, its descriptions are inescapably sexual and specific. 'How fair and how pleasant art thou, O love, for delights. This thy stature is like to a palm tree, and thy breasts to clusters of grapes.' Just an allegory? I don't think so. Indeed, so unavoidably suggestive is the text at times that some more prudish commentators have tried to airbrush it discreetly from the canon (the Mormons, for example, will have nothing to do with it), while others have used its imagery to deliver scholarly rulings on the acceptability of such sexual practices as oral sex between husbands and wives.

Sex matters. It's here to stay. And the world's religions realize this. They take sex seriously. How seriously you take it will determine the religion you choose and, similarly, how seriously you take your religion will determine the nature and frequency of the sex life you've chosen.

Command and control

While not every religion sees sex as a problem, all the world faiths recognize its power and, by extension, its dangers. As a result, they have drawn up elaborate rules to order and control it, to channel it, sometimes (as we have seen) to enhance it, and, in some circumstances, to curb it. But always to sanctify it.

The *Kama Sutra*, for example, is not an early forerunner of *The Joy of Sex*. It is not merely a sex manual. Sure, it explains half a dozen different ways to kiss, suggest more than 60 different sexual positions, and how to use your nails, teeth, tongue and hands to produce maximum satisfaction, but it is essentially a guide to the right and proper conduct between the sexes. So if you're thinking that life as a Hindu will just be chandeliers and sexy underwear, think again.

Judaism, Christianity and Islam, though different in their particulars, aren't that dissimilar in intention. They imply that, while there is a time for abandon, there is also a time for modesty and restraint. All three, however, maintain that the only place for sex is within heterosexual marriage. Judaism and Islam go further than Christianity in imposing abstinence even within marriage. In both traditions a husband and wife may not have sex while she is menstruating.

Rabbis stipulate a minimum of 12 days during which no sexual contact is permissible. After that time a Jewish woman visits a *mikveh*, or ritual bath, where immersion symbolically cleanses her of the taint of menstrual blood. Immediately afterwards sexual relations may resume. Those who follow the rules say that, far from denigrating the sexual act, such abstinence positively enhances it, freeing the couple to find other ways of expressing their love during this period of self-denial and building up the expectation of sensual pleasure after it has been observed. Moreover, couples are actively urged to have sexual intercourse on the Sabbath as an appropriate way of celebrating the day of rest.

In Islam, similarly, no genital contact may take place while the wife is menstruating but couples are encouraged to use other means such as kissing and caressing to demonstrate their affection. Sexual restraint in Jewish and Muslim teaching is not to be equated with prudishness or disgust whereas there is some evidence to suggest that historically this has been the case in Christianity.

It was arguably with St Paul that things got off to a negative start. In splitting off the body from the spirit and in relegating the physical to a vastly inferior role he downplayed the role of sexuality in human life. Even married love was a compromise, he seemed to argue, grudgingly recommending marriage only to those who couldn't keep their tunics on.

Such condescension towards the married state was consolidated in the fifth century CE when the theologian St Augustine of Hippo formulated a doctrine of Original Sin based on the pride and 'concupiscence' (selfish desire including sexual desire) of Adam and Eve. This led many to see sexuality as one of the principle causes of human sinfulness and, as such, in direct opposition to the strivings of the spirit. Although Augustine did not subscribe to such extremes he displayed a strong aversion to and suspicion of sexuality that has persisted into modern times. The fact that the monastic lifestyle incorporated chastity into its rulebook and that in the Roman Catholic Church celibacy became a requirement of the priesthood merely confirmed the essentially negative status of the body. Though, to be fair, that is not how most Catholic priests see it these days.

Judaism, by contrast, never had an ascetic tradition and, far from renouncing the sexual urge, embraced it as a vital component of married life. Moreover, married life itself was not a life choice but a divine injunction. Many Christian groups, perhaps learning from the Jewish way of life, are trying to rediscover the value of the physical in the worshipping lives of the faithful but they have a lot of misunderstanding and prejudice to unravel.

So those contemplating a religious life should take all these factors into consideration. They should also be prepared to renounce a life of promiscuity in favour of heterosexual married love, which, in Christian thinking, should be exclusive and for life. Both Judaism and Islam permit divorce and Islam allows a man to take up to four wives if he can provide materially for them all. Whatever the pleasures of the marital bed, however, there is to be no sex, in theory at least, until the wedding day (and, of course, no adulterous sex after it). This does, however, raise the question of what young people are to do before it.

The scriptures, remember, were written at a time when it wasn't unusual for people to marry at the age of 14. Nowadays 25 to 30 is nearer the mark (by which time in ancient societies you were almost certainly on the shelf and way past your prime). This leaves anything between

10 to 15 years of sexually mature life to motor through on a full tank of hormones and desire. What do you do short of inserting a cork or tying a knot in it? The scriptures aren't always clear, so it's been left to religious practitioners to infer some general rules from the text and devise systems to put them into practice.

Separation of the sexes from puberty onwards has been a classic way of solving the problem of sexual temptation. Christianity has tended to soft-pedal on this one, leaving Orthodox Judaism and Islam in the vanguard of sexual segregation whether in schools or places of worship.

Both Judaism and Islam have religious concepts of modesty and expect their adherents both to dress and behave in ways that are not likely to arouse sexual passions. You'll be expected to understand instinctively (or at least after some instruction) that men and women who are not close relatives are not expected to be alone together. This applies to some Anglican and Baptist churches, too, where you will ensure that a door is left open at all times if, at work, say, you and a member of the opposite sex are alone in discussion or interview.

Premarital sex is discouraged (in some Islamic countries it is punished harshly), but in the secular west where mixing of the sexes is inescapable if youngsters want to study and work in mainstream universities and businesses it cannot always be enforced. Religious leaders within all three Abrahamic traditions have had to accept that some sort of dating process is an inevitability for young people and to work hard to impress upon them the desirability of restraint. Hand holding, for example, is accepted even in otherwise strict Evangelical Christian congregations and even, though less so because one thing leads to another, kissing. The general guide is for young women to allow no touching 'between the neck and the knees' (which somewhat lacks the magisterial tenor of Mosaic commandment) and for young men to practise a sport like rugby or canoeing to take their mind off things.

But, as Marilyn said, sex is here to stay and even the wiser heads will often cross their fingers, not ask too many questions, and hope their sons and daughters get married as soon as possible. They'll also know and, if they really *are* wise, admit to themselves what they were like at their age. Masturbation (even if local canoeing facilities are oversubscribed) is not encouraged, but the days when priests and preachers forecast blindness or insanity as the inevitable consequence of the practice have largely gone. Though one Islamic website helpfully suggests those using pornography for arousal should try to bring to mind the torments of hell as described in the Koran rather than focusing on the images on the page. If pornography can be said to have a point (which in religious circles is debatable) this does rather miss it.

Homosexuality

The topic of same-sex relationships has divided and challenged many faiths and denominations and it seems reasonable to conclude that, where such divisions exist, no meeting of minds is going to be possible for many years to come. The orthodox historical position of all three of the Abrahamic faiths has been that homosexuality is not permissible (heterosexual marriage and procreation being the divinely ordained purpose of the sexual act). However, anyone considering Judaism and Christianity as religious options now has broadly traditional and broadly liberal wings to choose from. In line with the mores of the time, Progressive Judaism and liberal Christianity, for example, are generally accepting of practising gay people provided that their relationships are exclusive and not promiscuous. So far, Islam does not provide such 'liberal' options at anything like a formal level and continues to disapprove of homosexuality to the point of outlawing it as a capital offence in some communities.

Eastern religions, perhaps not surprisingly, take a more inclusive view. Straight or gay sex, in common with all other attachments to this world, is a potential snare and what matters more is the right attitude to such phenomena. On homosexuality per se, consequently, Buddhism is not nearly so specific either way.

Buddhist ethical principles are based on the consequences of one's actions. If these are primarily negative and lead to injury, guilt, shame or regret then the initial act is somehow deficient. If the results are positive, based on mutual consent, and lead to harmony and joy then the initial act is wholesome and does not interfere with the primary goal of nirvana, or enlightenment. This is not to give carte blanche to other sexual deviations from the mainstream. Adultery, paedophilia, promiscuity or exploitative sexual acts based on imbalances of power are not condoned by Buddhism, whereas consensual acts within a caring and supportive framework can be – whether those acts are heterosexual or homosexual in nature.

A world beyond

If you've been reading accounts of the hour-after-hour long sex sessions reputedly enjoyed by the rock star Sting and his wife and fancy some of that particular action, then so-called 'tantric sex' may be for you. But, as with all these ritual practices, they are not to be enjoyed overnight. They require pretty intense study and practice (no one's likely to complain about that, of course) but are not likely to be achieved if the sex alone is your desired goal. Heightened awareness of the source of divine energy is the goal. Sexual pleasure is the by-product.

Tantric practices are carried out within Hinduism and Buddhism and are normally performed by practitioners already well versed in both these respective religions. Such rites are often in tension with the mainstream Vedic and Buddhist traditions and certainly the Buddha himself consistently preached against magic, which some of the rituals (developed over five hundred years after his death) incorporate.

Essentially tantrism focuses on worship of the female energy (shakti) emanated by the Mother Goddess, Mahadevi. This energy is in opposition to the masculine energy of the god Shiva, while union of the two is said to have given birth to the whole of Creation. Accessing this source of divine power comes through the chakras (six centres of psychic energy said to be found at the base of the spine, in the genitals, in the navel, at the heart, at the throat and between the eyebrows).

Various schools of yoga activate this energy in different ways – ideally with a view to achieving spiritual liberation but most often, in a western context, for achieving a physical sense of well-being and vitality. Some tantric practices, however, employ *maithuna*, or sexual intercourse, as a vehicle for this liberation, its rhythmical movement reflecting the rhythmical vibration of the cosmos itself. Calm down at the back.

The female *shakti* energy is represented as a coiled snake or *kundalini* residing in the spinal chakra. It is said to be aroused by the arrest of breath and the retention of semen during the sexual act and spreads upwards through the chakras to a point just above the top of the head where union between the male–female polarities of the body takes place and the bliss of cosmic union ensues. In theory, the man stores up his semen, rather than expelling it through ejaculation. He also (and this is the tricky part) learns to absorb his partner's sexual fluid through his penis, prolonging sexual intercourse until he becomes like Shiva in physical union with the Goddess. Little wonder this takes a couple of hours. Traditionally, it is to be performed only under the supervision of an experienced guru.

Tantric exponents are sometimes divided into two camps: the right-hand path and the left-hand path (indicating the possible directions of travel of the *kundalini* up through the body). Some left-hand sects use extreme taboo-breaking practices to achieve spiritual communion, including living on cremation grounds, performing animal sacrifices, consuming meat and alcohol, and having sexual intercourse with menstruating women. It is thought that, in our especially decadent and dissolute age, ascetic practices are no longer effective and more extreme rituals are required. Those rituals that do make their way into the west from the cremation grounds of Calcutta probably do so in a suitably sanitized form. But probably best to ask Sting about that.

Tantric Buddhism is a similarly esoteric branch of mainstream Buddhism and is likewise taught stage by stage by tantric gurus who themselves are often celibate. The principle is to use sacramental ritual to channel energies through the body and thereby dissolve into a closer union with the Ultimate. The physical bliss that ensues is not the primary goal and anybody going into tantrism with that expectation in mind will be disappointed. As with the mystical branches of all the mainstream faiths, the goal is to use the body to transcend the body and thereby to enter into a greater spiritual communion. The net effects of such cosmic intercourse are, not surprisingly, spiritual, mental *and* physical.

Taoism, too, employs sexual and other physical rituals at its higher reaches, many of them influenced by tantric texts. Important are diet, exercise, personal hygiene and especially breath control, which is seen as one of the principal ways of mediating *ch'i*, the vital energy that is believed to pervade all things. One of Taoism's constants is the quest for immortality. This can be interpreted literally, metaphorically, or somewhere in between as a temporary postponement of death through longevity and increased vigour.

In common with tantric practices, retention of semen, suspension of orgasm and careful breath control are all techniques used to achieve this. Taoism also assigns oral sex a particular power in this regard. Those interested to see how this may have influenced popular art may like to take a look at Hokusai's woodblock print entitled *Dream of the Fisherman's Wife*. In it a gigantic octopus performs cunnilingus on a woman who, far from being startled or offended, is given over to blissful abandon and transported to a higher state. What St Augustine would have thought of it can only be imagined.

Secular sex, religious sex

Outside ancient Rome and Pompeii we in the west live in one of the most sexualized societies the world has seen. But arguably the sexual impulse has never before been so debased and pressed into service for such transparently commercial ends. Ubiquitous and alluring, it is used to sell everything from swimsuits to car parts, from newspapers to foreign holidays, and has lost the higher purpose the religions have traditionally sought to accord it.

The irony is that most people take the mistaken view that religion is puritanical about matters sexual and somehow embarrassed by them when, in reality, it is concerned with enhancing them, sanctifying them, and restoring them to their true purpose. Although procreation is a central part of this purpose, it is not the only part. It is also seen as a blessing provided by God for the mutual benefit and comfort of the married couple (the religions, for example, with the exception of Roman Catholicism, are broadly in favour of artificial contraception within marriage). Where the religions preach denial, self-control and occasional abstinence, they do so to ensure that the sexual impulse occupies what they see as its proper place in our lives; in balance and harmony with our other impulses and not directing and dominating them. In other words, in contrast to secular society's inducement to acquire more and more things and experience more and more sensations, religion seems to be saying that you can definitely have too much of a good thing.

1 **Hinduism** for its acceptance and celebration of human sexuality in its fullness. The *Kama Sutra* is a text that has no equivalent in world scripture. Written by the celibate Vatsyayana in the second century CE it is a practical guide to the erotic arts but always at the service of two higher ideals. The first is greater tenderness between human beings and the second is greater communion with the Godhead, the ultimate source of Creation. Each is at the service of the other. Travel some 400 miles south of New Delhi to Khajuraho and you will see an extraordinary temple complex dedicated to the Hindu deities. Among the thousands and thousands of intricately carved sculptures adorning the exterior you will see devotional scenes, scenes from everyday life, and scenes depicting uninhibited sexual activity between men and women, designed to be viewed without embarrassment or shame. Tourists should pack a pair of binoculars.

2 **Judaism** for its incorporation of the erotic into the everyday life of the married couple. Avoiding (though not necessarily excluding) the sexual fireworks that tantric sex is said to produce, it nonetheless hallows the pleasures of the marital bed and sees them as a direct gift of God. Indeed it is said that the *shekinah*, the spirit or presence of God, hovers over the marital bed during sexual intercourse, elevating an act of the body into one also of the spirit.

3 **Buddhism** for the tantric fireworks. Provided you can keep awake that long, which, with repeated practice of course, you will.

08

Food

The body as temple

You are now embarking on a tour of the world religions' rich and varied culinary traditions. You will not go hungry. Food is universally seen as a gift of God or the Gods, to be eaten with relish to feed the body, mind and spirit. Outside the rarefied domain of the ascetic's cell, food is to be celebrated not just as fuel to keep the body moving but as one of Creation's legitimate pleasures to be enjoyed with family, friends, strangers – and sometimes enemies – as a tangible sign of divine blessing.

Before you start licking your chops in anticipation, however, don't expect a kind of celestial eat-as-much-as-you-like buffet-style chow down. Yes, there'll be feasts and celebratory meals at festival times. But there'll also be fasts when discipline and self-denial will be required. And even in times of plenty you'll be expected to eat with restraint, not just shovelling it all in to satisfy your sensual cravings, but eating in moderation to remind yourself of life's higher purpose. The body, you'll be told, is a temple. Don't let it go to ruin.

Don't expect a smorgasbord either. You won't find everything served up on one platter. You may have to go to another part of the room for items that religious tradition demands should be served separately. In some traditions you'll find certain foods aren't served at all and you'll have to do without.

Food may be universal but diet is quite particular, conforming to the demands of a baffling permutation of rules and regulations. Here's your starter for ten. Why, even in the swankiest of restaurants, would Jews avoid the lobster linguine? Why would Muslims pass up a pork stir-fry. Why would a Sikh avoid the cheese omelette, why would a Hindu turn down a corned beef sandwich, and why would a Jain restaurant never serve you onion bhajis or carrot soup? You wouldn't think these were 'meaning of life' type questions. But you'd be wrong.

Thus spake the lord

Most of us, if we did but realize, dine like kings and queens compared to the 99.99 per cent of people who have gone before us. Our culinary options (in the prosperous west, at least) are exotic and varied beyond the wildest dreaming of our ancestors of even a hundred years ago. The average comfortably-off westerner growing up in any of the world's cities can dine at a different restaurant any night of the week and choose from a hitherto unimaginably vast array of food. In most centuries prior to our own, who but royalty could have enjoyed the levels of culinary sophistication we routinely enjoy as of right? From the spiced foods of the Far East, to out-of-season strawberries, from Neapolitan pizzas to the roast beef of Old England, we can have it all. Factor in the choc-ice and the Curly Wurly and even the courts of the Tudors and the Medici might be found wanting. We can simply help ourselves to it. And most of us do.

What the religions say, however, is just because it's there doesn't mean you can have it. Rules apply. Of the Abrahamic faiths, Judaism first codified them. There were (and continue to be) certain unclean foods that an observant Jew may not eat. These are defined by the so-called Kashrut ('fitting or proper') laws contained in the Book of Leviticus in the Hebrew Bible. Millions of scholarly words have been written on the Kashrut, or kosher, laws. Suffice it to say that if any of the following are on the menu you, as someone considering Judaism as a religion, will have to go hungry or dine elsewhere – pork, hare, camel (unlikely as a delicacy in the west, but you never know), lobster, oysters, shrimps, clams, prawns, crabs, frogs' legs and much more besides. Still, the list of approved foodstuffs is also quite long – beef, lamb, chicken, goose, duck, goat, venison, tuna, carp, salmon, herring, just for starters. You won't starve, that's for sure. But you will have to follow some general principles such as ensuring all meat has been slaughtered according to kosher practices (which forbid the pre-stunning of the beast) and meat and dairy products are not mixed. So while you can have a (kosher) Big Mac, a cheeseburger is out of the question.

The would-be Muslim has similar if more concise divine commands to follow: no carrion (not quite sure even Heston Blumenthal could rustle up a tasty supper with that, but that's a side issue), no blood products or pig, and no animal over which the name other than that of Allah has been pronounced. And, although the Koran mentions by name meat (repeat, no pork), dates, milk, fish, olives, pomegranates, seafood and figs, lots more food is potentially on your menu. There are two basic categories applying not only to food but to every aspect of human behaviour: that which is *halal* (permitted) and that which is *haram* (forbidden). Alcohol, by the way, is strictly *haram*.

Christianity, in contrast, has not sought to impose any similar dietary requirements or prohibitions except in relatively limited circumstances. The Apostle Paul (a fervently practising Jew until his conversion to Christ on the road to Damascus) declared that the ritual food practices of the Jews were now made redundant by the coming of the Messiah. Henceforth all food (provided it was collected, slaughtered, kept and prepared in self-evidently sanitary conditions) was permissible to the followers of Jesus. As he made clear in the First Letter to the Corinthians (12: 25–28), 'For the earth is the Lord's, and the fullness thereof. If any of them that believe not bid you to a feast, and you be disposed to go; whatever is set before you, eat, asking no question for conscience sake.' However even he proscribed food sanctified in the name of alien gods (a prohibition, as we have seen, taken up by the followers of Muhammad some six hundred years later). So the message for the potential Christian convert is simple – tuck in.

The vegetarian option

The religions of the east have their own dietary laws but show a broad measure of unanimity in avoiding meat. This is not for reasons of hygiene (which some say was the rationale behind steering clear of pork in the pre-refrigeration era of the Mediterranean and Middle East), but out of obedience to the religious principle of *ahimsa*, or non-violence, which has had a lasting influence on Hinduism, Buddhism and especially Jainism. So the ardent meat eater would be generally advised to give these religions a wide berth.

One of the best loved and most popular of the Hindu divinities is Lord Krishna, worshipped as the eighth incarnation of Vishnu the Sustainer. Among many of his accomplishments he also counted his skill as a cowherd and, as a result, his care for 'sacred cows' became a template for all Hindu devotees. Hence the ban on beef. If you want to see how strictly this is followed to this day, forget the streets of Delhi where cows wander unhindered, and instead take a trip to Hertfordshire and to Bhaktivedanta Manor, headquarters of the Hare Krishna movement in the UK. There you'll see state-of-the art cowsheds built of the finest oak beams, equipped with loudspeakers playing Sanskrit hymns to what must be the most cosseted herds of cattle in the country, if not the world. Twice a day the cows are milked until their producing days are over whereupon they are left in peace and retirement in the fields nearby. The devotees run the farm as a business and sell their 'Ahimsa Milk' to local shops and supermarkets where the discerning can literally get a taste of the Hindu way of life. Though it's not cheap. In fact, at around £3 a litre, it's the most expensive milk in the country – and you can see why.

Hardeep Singh Kohli (b. 1969), Scottish Sikh writer and broadcaster

*For me food is about people. With the exception of Judaism I can't think of a religion where **food is so central to the faith**. Food in the Sikh faith is part of worship. In Sikhism there is such a thing a free lunch – thanks to the langar, the* communal kitchen serving free food to everybody. So the richest woman in society will sit down with the poorest. And it's important for me that the food is prepared by the **community**, volunteers of every age working together preparing food provided by voluntary donations. When I was a kid growing up in Glasgow I'd see people turning up at the gurdwara with bags of potatoes or punnets of mushrooms. That's **egalitarianism** and for me it's one of the single defining tenets of the faith.

I am interested in the culture of Sikhism, which is unarguably driven by that sense of a higher power which is God but – and I'll be shot down in flames for this – I don't think you need to believe in God to be a Sikh. What I love about Sikhism is its commitment to **social justice**. We are a religion born out of an attempt to redress the balance of social injustice and I feel empowered by my faith to stand up for those who are not able to stand up for themselves. I went to law school and trained as a barrister for that reason.

Ironically, we are probably the best business people and free marketeers you'll meet, but at heart we are a **socialist** religion. It was interesting growing up in the west of Scotland and noticing the Protestant work ethic. The Sikh **work ethic** is that for us work is worship. I was educated at a Jesuit school and I noticed a great crossover between their Catholicism and the Sikh faith in that both of them have a commitment to social egalitarianism.

The thing I love about the Sikh faith most is that it's **non-evangelical**. We genuinely believe that if our religion is so good, people will come to it. And one of the mantras I grew up with from my parents was 'It's better to be a good person than a bad Sikh.'

Buddhists, too, adhere to a vegetarian diet and, if you're planning on this way of life, start to develop a taste for beans, pulses, fruit and nuts to accompany your veg. But don't start developing too much of a taste, for the Buddha recommended simplicity in eating, avoiding pungent smells, strong aromas, rich sauces and the things that invite sensual attachment. In short, all the things that make food tasty to the western palate.

Zen Buddhist monks at the 500-year-old Hwa Gye Sah Temple in Seoul, South Korea, for example, rise at around 3 a.m. and begin their daily discipline of meditation. They break for breakfast (generally eaten in silence) of rice, soup, pickled vegetables, cucumbers, spinach and mung beans and then resume prayer and meditation. Lunch is much the same (rice and soup) and that's usually it for the day with the exception of perhaps a rice cake and a bowl of tea. Let's face it, it's going to be some years before the beginner will get into that routine but that's broadly the sort of self-discipline you're aiming at eventually.

But if you're considering going down the Jain path of spirituality be prepared for an even more radical reappraisal of your western culinary expectations. Because something of the ascetic way of life is expected of both the layperson and the monk or nun, the diet is demanding in the extreme – vegetarianism, of course, for fear of harming any living creature, but also no roots or tubers that sprout into life and whose removal from the ground can kill tiny insects and micro-organisms invisible to the naked eye. In other words, it's vegetarianism, Jim, but not as we know it. No potatoes, garlic, onions, carrots, swedes, turnips and so on and no eating after sunset when organisms might sprout on your food and bugs might be attracted to the light you're eating it by. Still think you can hack it? Oh, and no honey either.

What you'll get in return, however (all other things being equal), is a life progressively refined of the negative karma holding back your spiritual progress. Unlike the Hindu and Buddhist concept of karma (the moral law of the universe), Jains consider it to be like fine particles of matter that adhere to the soul as mud sticks to a shoe, holding back your progress towards *moksha*, or release from the ongoing cycle of birth, death and rebirth. This really is soul food and, let's face it, it's a rather more persuasive inducement to eating your greens than being told they'll put hairs on your chest or make your hair curl.

And if vegetarianism presents you with no problems then other religious options are spread out before you, too. Taoism, Confucianism, Zoroastrianism, the Baha'i faith, and, moving further westwards, Neopaganism, Druidry and Rastafarianism all tend, in varying degrees, towards the veggie option, though not exclusively. Confucius, for example, is said to have been rather partial to ginger in summer and turnips in winter (takes all sorts) but recommended chopping meat finely to aid digestion. Rastafarians, who follow a regime known as *ital* to promote vital energy or 'livity', are inclined towards a vegetarian diet (certainly avoiding pork and shellfish) but might just be partial to the Jamaican classic of ackee and salt fish. Much as they might be tempted, they wouldn't wash it down with a cold beer, as alcohol (along with fizzy drinks, tea, coffee and other stimulants) is banned. Many Druids, with ecological concerns for the protection of Mother Earth, avoid foods with artificial flavours and chemical preservatives and, while not exclusively vegetarian, incline towards free-range and organic processes of meat rearing.

If you're drawn to Sikhism, the only meat you'll be absolutely forbidden from eating is that derived from ritual slaughter. Accordingly both kosher and halal meat are off the menu. Traditionally, Sikhs were encouraged not to eat beef or pork anyway for fear of giving offence to their Hindu or Muslim neighbours. And so it is today that, out of exquisite good manners and culinary courtesy, only vegetarian food is served in the *langar*, or communal kitchen of the gurdwara. That way no one stopping by for food will be embarrassed or offended.

Festivals, fasts and feasts

If food is woven into the fabric of the religious way of life, it's hardly surprising that it's going to be integral to the high days and holy days that punctuate the religious calendar. It will also be incorporated into the religious routines of everyday life.

It is, after all, with a Friday night meal that the Jewish Sabbath is ushered in, the wine symbolizing the sweetness and joy of this special day and the plaited loaf of bread symbolizing the double portion of manna given to the Israelites in the wilderness after the Exodus from Egypt. Bolshie adolescents who'd prefer to spend Friday nights with their mates somewhere else may find this weekly requirement irksome (though rabbis and Jewish youth workers are working heroically to find ways of making the Sabbath attractive during the dreaded teenage years), but if you are of the *right* age (whatever that is) you will enjoy this shared meal in a way you never would a takeaway in front of the telly.

Christians celebrate their Sabbath worship with a rite known variously as the Eucharist, Holy Communion, the Lord's Supper, the Blessed Sacrament, the Divine Liturgy, the Breaking of Bread and other terms. This symbolizes the Last Supper when Jesus instructed his disciples to take bread and wine in memory of his body and blood. Not a meal in any conventional sense it nonetheless is at the core of Christian devotional practice and, in a way that is at once tangible and mysterious, connects Christians today to the historical and momentous events of two thousand years ago.

Likewise, at Passover, Jews hold a Seder to commemorate the events of the Exodus. The evening incorporates both an actual and a symbolic meal, the latter comprising bitter herbs to symbolize the harshness of slavery, a paste of fruit and nuts to symbolize the mortar the Jewish slaves mixed for the pharaohs, salt water to symbolize their tears, and a lamb shank bone and a roasted egg to symbolize Temple sacrifice. In addition, four cups of red wine are drunk, symbolizing not only the four promises of redemption made by the Almighty but the lamb's blood that marked the Jewish houses 'passed over' by the spirit of the Lord and thus spared from the direst of the Plagues of Egypt.

Just as there is a time for eating so, too, you will find there is a time for fasting. So be prepared – as a mark of self-discipline and interior reflection on the divine plan – to go without food from time to time.

Muslims are expected to forgo food and drink between sunrise and sunset during the holy month of Ramadan, which commemorates the month when God chose Muhammad as His Prophet and sent down the revelations of the Koran. You will not starve during this month, though if it falls outside the short days of winter and occurs during the longer days of summer (Islam being a religion that follows a shifting lunar calendar) it will be a testing discipline indeed.

Christians have an equivalent month of self-sacrifice and reflection during the 40 days of Lent leading up to Easter. Lent is not codified in the same way as Ramadan and nowadays it is left to the individual's conscience to decide what food or drink to renounce (though alcohol and chocolate are popular – or, rather, unpopular – choices).

Fasting is obligatory on the holiest day of the Jewish year, Yom Kippur, or the Day of Atonement, which is the culmination of ten days of penitence ushered in by Rosh Hashanah, the Jewish New Year.

What unites all these symbolic occasions is food – or the lack of it. If you're thinking about taking the religious path bear in mind that, while food nourishes the body, on special occasions its absence nourishes the soul.

For God's sake read the label

It's easy to think that, if you're planning to become religious, all you have to do in dietary terms is avoid specific foods – variously pork chops, black puddings, prawn curries, egg sandwiches, beef dripping, garlic bread, or a myriad of other recognizable dishes that you could photograph and attach to your fridge with a magnet. Oh, if only it were that simple. But it isn't.

The new convert to most religions will soon learn that it is not just the food itself but all the derivatives from the food that count just as much. And in this day and age when we are used to countless natural and artificial sweeteners, flavourings, colourings and preservatives, unseen dangers lurk in even the most superficially innocuous of substances. A jelly for a Jewish children's party may contain gelatin made from pig's bones, a stock cube for a Hindu vegetable curry may contain beef extract, pastries for a Jain buffet or a Buddhist reception may contain cochineal dye from the crushed wings of a cactus-eating insect, a splash of soy sauce may contain alcohol. You get the idea.

With enzymes, rennets, wheys, E numbers and additives of every conceivable sort potentially hiding in your store cupboard without your knowing, you're going to have to do quite a bit of culinary research to stay on the right side of many religious laws. But fear not – as you will be able to rely on a band of religious food detectives who will track down offending items and alert you and your fellow faithful to their presence in your shopping trolleys. It'll take time and effort but you'll be rewarded in good time. For the purpose of all this bother is to enable you to eat well … and to be healthy not only in body but in mind and in spirit. And who wouldn't drink – or eat – to that?

TOP THREE ★★★

1 **Christianity** for its licence to be omnivorous. Fish and fowl, game and greens, meat and two veg. It's all divinely sanctioned and all on the menu. No food is intrinsically unclean and no permutation of foodstuffs prohibited. This doesn't mean you'll be handed a licence to gorge yourself silly. Proper restraint and self-denial are in order at all times and are expected at key dates in the worshipping calendar – notably in the periods of self-reflection of Lent and Advent leading up to Easter and Christmas respectively. However, in Britain at least, Christianity has certainly had to up its culinary game to keep pace with the delicacies provided by the joint holders of the number 3 slot.

2 **Sikhism** for the unique institution of the *langar*, the communal kitchen at the heart of the gurdwara offering a community resource for the brother- and sisterhood of Sikh believers, providing a focal point for friendship and sharing, and dispensing free food for the needy of every creed, colour or class.

3 **Islam** and **Hinduism** for the spicy concoctions that grace practically every high street in the land. Chicken jalfrezi with pilau rice, lamb rogan josh with flatbreads, a sumptuous vegetarian thali fit for a prince or a manual labourer. Divine.

09

Clothes

Clothes maketh the man

It's reckoned that the British fashion industry alone is worth nearly 21 billion pounds a year, fuelled by men and women wanting to stand out from the crowd, make a splash, and show to the world their individuality and flair. From that figure you can safely conclude that globally the rag trade is worth squillions of pounds, dollars, euros, roubles and rupees.

But, not surprisingly, none of that turnover is provided by the saints and holy men of India's Digambara sect of Jainism. Why? For the simple reason that they don't wear clothes. Not a stitch. Naked as the day they were born, they renounce everything apart from the bare essentials, as it were, needed to survive, leading the life of homeless wanderers, and relying on charity for their food. They may possess one scrap of cloth to filter their daily drink of water – not for their own sake but to prevent insects and living organisms from being swallowed by accident – but beyond that they possess nothing. And consequently birthday suits are the order of the day. At least for male ascetics. Nakedness is deemed inappropriate for women, who must wait until they are reborn as men to be able to practise this particular brand of sartorial renunciation. Anywhere else but in India you'd get arrested for it. Frankly anywhere else but in India you'd pretty soon feel the cold. Either way, this dramatic gesture is greeted with neither outrage nor surprise by the naturally devout population of the subcontinent. Instead they recognize that some individuals feel the need to make this bold and highly visible statement as part of their lifetime commitment to freeing themselves from all attachment to people and things.

'Clothes maketh the man,' said the nineteenth-century American humorist Mark Twain. 'Naked people have little or no influence on society.' Well, up to a point, old boy. And an exception is arguably Mahatma Gandhi, who, though not a Jain himself, grew up among Jains and did more than anyone to spread the message of non-violence (the *ahimsa* so central to Jain philosophy), first across a continent then across the world. But we digress. So here's an option from the outset. Do you fancy becoming a 'sky-clad' Jain monk? Just think, you'd never have to worry about your wardrobe again.

One more fashion statistic. Leaving the British figure distinctly in the shade, the Islamic fashion industry is reckoned to generate 96 billion dollars worldwide every year. With Digambara Jains at one end of the spectrum and fashionably devout Muslims at the other, it's clear that dress (or the lack of it) counts for much in religious thinking. So which religion are you inclined to plump for if you're motivated by a sense of style?

Humility and modesty

The first thing to bear in mind is that, generally speaking, more will be asked of you if you are a woman. Restrictions on male attire do apply and can be exceedingly strict, but in purely numerical terms more men than women are given the latitude to dress broadly as they wish – and more in tune with the secular mainstream.

The second thing to consider if you're picking a religion with its dress code in mind (and this is pretty much universal) is that, in complete opposition to secular fashion where individual style and ostentation are prized above all else, humility in dress will be your guiding principle. God or enlightenment is your ultimate goal and anything that takes your eye off the spiritual ball will not be appropriate.

So the Anabaptist Christian sects of sixteenth-century Europe, in stressing their nonconformity to the mainstream practices of the day, turned their backs on everything from voting and giving evidence in court to the wearing of wedding rings (and, of course, to infant baptism). Pretty soon their dress mirrored this, too. And their heirs today – the Amish, the Mennonites, the Bruderhof, the Brethren, the Hutterites and other sub-sects – encourage personal humility and separation from the world by the very clothes they wear.

The Amish, for example, follow Henry Ford's motto for his Model T: 'Any colour as long as it's black.' At least for 'black' read 'dark' (though you should forget about having a car on the farm – or a telephone, or a television, or a radio for that matter). Suits are dark in colour and plain in cut, without lapels, buttons or pockets. Shirts are usually plain blue or white and can have buttons, while jackets have to rely on hooks and eyes. Belts, sweaters, ties and gloves are forbidden. If you're wondering how men keep their trousers up in Lancaster County, Pennsylvania, then think braces (or 'suspenders' as they're usually called in those parts), which are said to smack more of plain utility than of the personal ornamentation associated with the belt. The ensemble is topped off with a broad-brimmed black felt or straw hat – which to the outsider can look effortlessly stylish. Though, of course, that is definitely *not* the idea and many Amish are uneasy that theirs is becoming 'a look'.

Women generally wear long-sleeved, unpatterned dresses with ankle or calf-length skirts (the length often strictly prescribed by community elders) and an apron. On their heads they wear a simple bonnet and top this off with a cape covering the head and shoulders. Shoes and stockings are black. So, ladies, prepare to dress as plainly as the menfolk and remember that neither jewellery nor make-up is permitted.

Though different in their particulars, Amish styles promote a mindset that is shared by all the world's religions – that personal vanity is inimical to spiritual growth.

But if humility is a guiding principle so, too, is modesty. Those considering becoming full members of any religion should bear this in mind from the outset and be prepared to accept limitations to what mainstream society routinely allows – and, if the fashion magazines are anything to go by, actively encourages. There will be adjustments – quite possibly sacrifices – but the idea is to lose something of yourself in order to gain much, much more.

Islam is no different. So, taking its cue from the Koran, it is very hot on modesty. What's confusing, however, is the variety of interpretations governing actual practice. Different communities across the world have different traditions and, to the outsider, it's not always easy to distinguish purely cultural practices from what is formally required by the faith. Somali Muslim women, for example, may wear a *chador*, a large cape covering their head and upper body (much the same as Amish women and Christian nuns), but they often keep their face uncovered. Many Saudi women cover all but the eyes whereas others in Afghanistan may choose (or be forced) to wear the all-encompassing *burqa*, the shuttlecock-like body covering that renders the woman invisible to any passing gaze. So much so that several years ago the burly six-foot BBC World Affairs correspondent John Simpson was able to disguise himself in one and slip across the Afghan border undetected.

But whether *chador*, *burqa*, *shalwar*, *kameez* (the long tunic teemed with baggy trousers) or *jilbab* (the full-length tailored robe) the unifying feature is their looseness. Anything that hugs the contours of the body or that is flimsy or transparent is deemed immodest and, by extension, un-Islamic.

While debate abounds in Islamic circles over the desirability of one item of clothing over another, opinion is pretty much uniform on the *hijab*, the headscarf covering a woman's hair. Muslim legalists are keen to stress that such rules are in place to demonstrate obedience to God rather than to suggest submissiveness to men. The *hijab* is worn largely willingly and without question and is usually the least that is required of a devout Muslim woman in the way of dress code. Many practising women in the west and elsewhere, however, do elect not to wear one and consider themselves just as much a Muslim as anyone else.

Different rules apply to Muslim men, who must remain covered from the navel to the knee and who are forbidden from wearing tight, revealing, or excessively eye-catching clothes. In addition, they should not wear silk or sport gold jewellery, and avoid the colour yellow on the grounds that all these things are deemed effeminate. One particularly severe interpretation of what the Prophet intended is to be found in one Hadith stating that hellfire awaits any man wearing trousers that come down below the ankles. Even for those familiar with the term 'fashion crime' this seems just a little excessive – though interestingly enough a similar prohibition is still on the statute book for Orthodox Jews, whose trouser bottoms must on no account sweep the floor. The religions have many things in common but, being honest for a moment, who'd have thought that trouser length was one of them? Equally who'd have thought a couple of inches of suit material could spell the difference between heaven and hell?

Arguably the most heated debate, however, surrounds women's wearing of the *niqab*, the face veil obscuring everything but the eyes. Supporters of this (many of them young women born and raised in the west) say that not only is it Islamically ordained but that it is a lifestyle choice freeing them from the tyranny of being treated as a sexual object by men. Critics disagree and point out that Muhammad himself made it clear to his followers that a woman's face and hands need not be covered. Not only that, they go on to suggest that in insisting on something over and above what the Prophet ordained some women are effectively considering themselves to be better and more devout believers than their Muslim sisters – an arrogant assumption that comes perilously close to the sin of pride.

Obeying the rules

You may have guessed by now that, from the moment you opt for a religion, getting dressed in the morning is not going to be the same as it used to be. No more just putting on what's lying on the floor. No more repeat visits to the mirror to see if this or that outfit or these or those boots look right. It's not going to be the same but in some ways it's going to be easier. You're not going to have to think about what to wear because by and large the thinking will have already been done for you and all *you* have to do is follow the rules.

For the Amish those rules are contained in the Ordnung, the list of written and oral rules outlining the basics of Amish belief and practice and defining what it means to be Amish. In Islam, the rules come from the Koran and the

Hadiths. In Judaism, they come from the first five books of the Hebrew Bible, collectively known as the Torah, and from the interpretations of the Torah contained in the Talmud.

Orthodox Jews are punctilious in observing the rules (ten big ones, of course, but 613 others known as *mitzvah, singular mitzvot* which govern every aspect of daily life including dress). These they divide into laws that can be explained and understood rationally and laws that can't be understood. No matter whether you get them or you don't (and that's partly where the rabbis come in, devising learned interpretations for the rank and file), you have to follow them.

So, get used to ditching that favourite suit of yours if it's made of a wool mix. *Shatnez* it's called and it's forbidden. Rabbis have argued that the reason you may not mix wool and fabric or flax goes back to Genesis and to the two offerings the brothers Cain and Abel brought to the Lord, one of wool, one of flax. And look what a kerfuffle that caused. So better not do it. The interpretation may be disputed and the real reason may never be known. But the point is you don't *need* to know why. You simply have to do it because *it says so* in the text (Deuteronomy 22:11).

Likewise the *tzitzit*, the fringes or tassels on the edges of the prayer vest that can often be seen protruding at the waist beneath the (white) shirt of an Orthodox Jewish man. Why they have to be worn is far from obvious but that they do is a given because, as before, *it says so* in the scripture (Deuteronomy 22:12 and Numbers 15:38). And don't, at least to begin with, enquire about the number of threads and knots required to make up these fringes unless you have a few hours to spare to devote to the intricacies of numerology in the Kabbalah. For the record, the *tzitzit* is assigned a numerical value of 600 (don't ask), each tassel has eight threads and five knots and the total comes to 613, the exact number of *mitzvot* that have to be carried out. Simple when you know. Surplus to everyday requirements when you don't.

But perhaps the most distinctive item you'll have to get used to wearing if Orthodox Judaism is for you is the *kippah*, aka the *yarmulke* or skull cap, worn on its own or, more often than not, under a larger, broad brimmed homburg or fedora. The homburg is a cultural and optional accessory (replaceable for married men in some communities by wide fur hats suggestive of crowns and Middle European nobility) but the *kippah* (or a head covering of some sort) is a spiritual 'must have'. According to the Talmud the head must be covered at all times when walking more than a few yards as a reminder that the fear of the divine presence is always above.

Some ultra-Orthodox communities may insist on a more distinctive dress code. For example, they may insist on white socks or stockings tucked under breeches. They may also fasten buttons right over left in conformity to Kabbalistic requirements (again don't ask) or favour the wearing of outfits traditionally worn in Middle European communities in the eighteenth century. And, on a possibly jarring note for the fashion-conscious, Orthodox Judaism does seem to insist on sandals *with* socks.

However, many of the above are required only in closer-knit communities or on special occasions. The average Orthodox Jew on the bus or Tube can be recognized by the more usual white shirt, dark suit and dark overcoat with a hat (or maybe two) and will not stand out excessively from the crowd – especially given what lots of people wear on the Tube these days. But stand out he will. Because that is the point of religious dress. It is designed to make you stand out and, as we shall see in a moment, designed to make you different. Being to a greater or lesser degree apart from the mainstream is an integral part of the deal. Be prepared for it.

Very like their Amish counterparts, women wear long skirts and tops with sleeves past the elbow. They, too, cover their heads (beanies and berets are popular) but, whereas Amish women grow their hair long and tie it in a bun, married Jewish women cut their hair short and wear a wig.

If you feel you're more attracted to Progressive or non-Orthodox Judaism, dress codes are not so prescriptive. You will find yourself wearing the kind of suits, jackets, ties, skirts and dresses worn by most people in the wider non-Jewish world, but, if you're a man, it's wise to keep a *kippah* handy for synagogue visits.

Belonging to the club

Religious dress, as we've seen, is a visible metaphor for spirituality and for such virtues as modesty and humility but it's also designed as a badge of allegiance to the group.

If you like the idea of becoming a Rastafarian, for example, you'll more than likely start to cultivate the dreadlocks immediately – not only for the spiritual associations they have with the Lion of Judah (symbol of the ancient Israelite tribe whose descendants are believed by Rastas to be the African people) but to show that you belong. Everything from your bearing to your diet will proclaim this but perhaps nothing so visibly as the red, gold, green and black *tam* on your head into which you will tuck your flowing mane.

Similarly when the Sikhs' tenth guru, Gobind Singh, founded the community of warrior saints and baptised them into the 'pure' order of the Khalsa with *amrit* (nectar or sweetened water) he devised for them a code of dress that would make them stand out in a crowd. Henceforth, by the very way they looked, they would be known as a band of brothers united in their commitment to helping and protecting the weak against the potential tyranny of the strong. The symbolism persists to this day and fully baptised Sikhs wear or carry the emblems of the so-called Five Ks. These are the *kara* (the steel bangle), the *kanga* (the comb), the *kachera* (baggy shorts), the *kirpan* (ceremonial dagger) and, perhaps most distinctive of all, the *kech* – the uncut hair wrapped in the turban.

To wear the turban is to be *visible*, to be marked out inescapably as a member of the club, and to display with pride your spiritual associations. And there's no doubting it can look exceedingly smart. To see the Glasgow comedian and gourmet Hardeep Singh Kohli turning up at a Burns Night supper, say, wearing a tartan kilt and a pale pink turban is not just to appreciate a stunning fashion statement but to witness an expression of pride in and belonging to the group (in Hardeep's case to *two* groups).

However, you could get the same sense of belonging were you to consider practising as a Buddhist monk. The simple saffron robes of the Theravada school of Buddhism prevalent in Thailand, Cambodia, Laos and Sri Lanka are in part designed to foster just such a sense. In decreeing that all his followers should wear those orange robes the Buddha declared:

> Liberation is not attained when we are acting in our own capacity and for our own interest. Liberation is attained when we give up our personal identity and enter into a bigger story. Then we merge with the sangha [Buddhist community] and are all of one appearance without rank or pride.

You might choose to don the black, blue, brown or grey robes of Mahayana Buddhism prevalent in Japan, China and South Korea but, either way, you will be visibly affiliating yourself to a group, a tribe, a club, a team.

Ceremonial dress vs the everyday

It is one thing to belong to the religious elite of ordained monks and nuns; quite another to practise the faith as a layperson. Most Buddhists look no different from the mainstream of whichever society they belong to. Neither do the majority of ordinary rank-and-file Hindus, Jains or Druids for that matter. You may find patterns of dress emerging, however, in looser-fitting clothes that facilitate the flow of energy through the body, in earth colours, and non-synthetic fabrics that are in harmony with the natural world. Druids, for example, may have a penchant for wearing loose kaftans, shawls and capes and avoid wearing fur or leather but hard-and-fast rules don't always apply. Crushed velvet, though, never seems to go out of favour.

Similarly if you're planning to become a Hindu you will have to ditch the leather shoes and stick to natural materials. Outside the Indian subcontinent, the *dhoti*, the large unstitched rectangular sheet wrapped round the legs, waist and shoulders, is not a common garment and certainly in Britain is not seen outside the priestly class officiating in temple worship. However, a modified form of the *dhoti* when teamed with a smart knee-length close fitting tunic known as the *sherwani* is always a hit on ceremonial occasions, especially at Hindu and Sikh weddings.

For Hindu women the sari is pretty much universal though, for the younger generation of British-born Hindus, it's not a cultural requirement. Western dress, provided it is modest and discreet, need not be in opposition to Hinduism's core values. Interestingly, though, the sari, the single length of cloth wound round the body and worn with a *choli*, or short blouse ending below the bust, allows for a degree of bare flesh that is deemed neither erotic nor provocative. Elderly ladies who could be your grandmother or favourite aunt routinely dress in this way without remotely causing offence or comment. Nakedness and nudity, it seems, are all in the mind.

In all religious communities dressing appropriately is a common feature and something summed up perhaps in the phrase deriving from Christian practice in Britain, the 'Sunday best'. You will almost certainly find that precisely *what* you wear is less important than the sense of cleanliness, care and pride with which you wear it, but in many Christian communities Sunday is definitely a day to wear something special for the Lord's sake. In some rural Calvinist congregations in Scotland, say, this will involve sober and severe styles dominated largely by dark colours whereas in many African or Afro-Caribbean Pentecostal churches in the big cities you'll see bright clothes and exuberant colours – not for vanity's sake but in joyful celebration of the Lord's day. So, ladies, if you're fond of elaborate hats and bright multi-patterned head coverings, then these congregations will definitely be for you.

Liturgical dress is, again, another matter and priestly garb is a specialist subject in itself. You might like to check up on the alb, the amice, the cincture, the chasuble, the surplice, the dalmatic, the buskins and the cope (alternatively you might not) to see exactly what the well-dressed priest, bishop, cardinal or pope is wearing, but it won't necessarily advance your appreciation of the wearer's inner spiritual status. As in other traditions, the symbolism is extensive – from the number of buttons on a priest's cassock to the red shoes worn by the Pope himself – but they are only the outward signs.

Far more important, of course, is whether they serve an inner devotion.

And, for the record, the Pope's shoes *are* red (to symbolize martyrdom and the blood of Christ) but they are *not* made by Prada. That privilege belongs to a Roman family firm of shoemakers.

As for lay Christians, these days there's a relaxed view about what exactly one's Sunday best means. Certainly, the younger generation of Christians dresses no different from their secular counterparts and considers – in the end, quite soundly – that goodness and faithfulness reside in people's hearts not in their outward uniforms.

Holiness and separation

The ancient Hebrew word for 'holy' also carries another meaning that can roughly be translated as 'apart' or 'separate'. And this may be a difficult concept for many people to accept. It means to some degree leaving people, places, things and lifestyles behind to set yourself apart from your old life in order to begin anew. And to every benefit there is a cost.

Take the Muslim headscarf. Women may feel distinctly odd when they first wear it, for example, and they will initially feel quite apart from the hurly-burly of the high street or the shopping precinct. In time, though, first-hand reports suggest that it will feel unexpectedly exhilarating. In return for the partial loss of self is the arguably greater gain of community and belonging. Christian nuns and Amish women in their bonnets feel exactly the same. So do Orthodox Jews. The *kippah* and the fringes, the wig and the long dresses, all mark the wearer out as someone different. Someone who is trying to be holy.

So there you have it, a variety of styles to choose from, a variety of faiths to pick. Adopting one will almost certainly come as a culture shock. But remember that, if some of these religious styles seem restrictive and designed to stifle any individual creative spark, this is not what they were intended to do. On the contrary, believers will tell you they exist not to restrict but to liberate.

Clothes are meant to be part of the spiritual machinery that will free you from your attachments to the things that will pass away and concentrate your mind and heart on the things that will endure. Personal vanity, it is argued, keep you shackled to the fashions and illusions of the age and these will surely fade, while humility and service to God will open for you a door to a spiritual life that will abide for evermore.

And as Harrison Ford and Kelly McGillis proved in the unforgettable Amish-based thriller *Witness*, all those years ago, some people can look good in anything.

TOP THREE ★★★ ★★

1 **Hinduism:** the infinitely adaptable sari combines relaxed formality with an understated sense of inner piety. And for men what could be smarter than a beautifully tailored *sherwani* and the timeless Nehru jacket of the Indian aristocracy?

2 **Black Pentecostal Christianity:** the unrestrainedly vibrant colours worn by women in the congregations lift the spirits on dark winter days and put joy back into worship. Also their sons or brothers or nephews on duty inside and outside the church invariably look great in their sharp suits, too.

3 **Sikhism:** the appeal of a man in uniform has been said to be significant. But this uniform (especially the turban) manages to be both lofty and noble while at the same time making a reassuringly approachable and friendly impression.

NEAR MISS →

Islam: the $96 million has got to be partly wasted as long as the *niqab* and the *burqa* obscure a woman's face. But the clean minimalist lines of some of the outfits are extraordinarily elegant. The *jilbab* worn by Keanu Reeves in *The Matrix Reloaded*, for example, is truly something else.

10 Money

Faith and the folding stuff

The next time you get a tax demand bear in mind you've the Book of Deuteronomy in the Hebrew Bible to thank for it. It won't get you a rebate from the taxman but it will put your anguish into a historical context. It's from this book of ancient wisdom among others that we've drawn our principles of financial mutuality, of contributing to a community chest that will meet the needs and wants of a society. Deuteronomy is also the basis for bankruptcy law and the bedrock on which every charity from ActionAid to the Zimbabwe National Emergency Fund rests. The scriptures have a lot to say about how we order a just and caring society and they recognize that money is a part of it.

'Money is the root of all evil,' I hear you say, so how can the religions mix money and godliness? But, of course, this is one of the most widely *misquoted* texts in the Bible. In his First Letter to Timothy (6:10 for the record) Paul actually says, 'For love of money is the root of all evil, which while some coveted after, they have erred from the faith, and pierced themselves through with many sorrows.' In other words money is like fire, useful but dangerous. Though they express themselves in different terms, all the religions agree on this: while we need money to order the daily transactions of our lives, excessive interest in it not only cuts us off from God but makes us unhappy into the bargain.

But the religious texts have much more to say about the cash in our pockets and bank accounts. So, if you're considering joining a religion it's as well to know what you'll be letting yourself in for and do a bit of financial calculation up front to see whether you feel you can hack it.

For all the benefits you'll derive from Jewish family and social life, for example, you'll need to be prepared to be 10 per cent worse off financially. Likewise, Christian discipleship will theoretically cost you around a tenth of your taxed income – in addition to what you stump up week by week for the church collection. Would-be Muslims confront the same religious duty and should be ready to give away around 2.5 per cent of their net worth.

Not only that, as a devout Muslim you'll find it very difficult to rent a car and not at all straightforward to buy a house. Why? Because to rent a car you'll need a credit card and to buy a house you'll need a mortgage – and on both of these transactions you'll be charged interest, which is forbidden in the Koran. Such is the ubiquity of credit cards these days that some Muslim scholars have argued that they are a regrettable necessity in the modern western world and have sanctioned their use in limited circumstances. Provided the faithful stop short of racking up a whopping balance and use their card with restraint, they argue that credit cards have become an unavoidable compromise they have to make in predominantly non-Muslim societies.

Wherever possible, Muslim leaders advise seeking out alternatives to loans and interest and recommend dealing with the increasing number of financial institutions operating according to Sharia, or Islamic law. In the case of a house purchase this might involve agreeing to buy the property jointly with the bank and month by month pay an agreed sum which is part rent and part repurchase of the bank's share of the transaction. It will, almost certainly cost you more than taking out a conventional mortgage but at least you'll be able to sleep in the house at night with a clear conscience.

In both Judaism and Christianity usury or charging disproportionate levels of interest was also considered a sin. Making money merely from the passage of time when that time could be spent not on worrying about repayment but on focusing on God was thought to be a form of blasphemy. But from time to time people would inevitably find themselves in financial need that only a loan could assuage. What then? In those cases money-lending was seen as a form of philanthropy. Accordingly, Jews were forbidden from charging interest on loans made to fellow Jews but could do so on those made to Gentiles. In medieval Europe Jews were barred from entering the trades and professions of the Christian majority so were banished to the fringes of society and into the marginal but necessary occupations shunned by Christians. Money-lending was one of them and it became yet another excuse for anti-Semitic prejudice. In time, however, Gentile bankers of the Renaissance, such as the Lombards and the Medici, would come to charge far higher levels of interest than the Jews and no one batted an eyelid. But that is perhaps another story.

The cost of discipleship

In choosing to embark on the religious life you will be choosing to help and care for your fellow human beings. That much is a given. Misanthropes need not apply. So where will your responsibilities lie and how should you discharge them?

In Judaism the act of charitable giving is known as *tzedakah*, which has at its root the idea of righteousness. Not only is helping others seen as a natural human impulse, it also carries with it an implied spiritual blessing on the giver who is reassured that he or she is doing God's commandments. The mere handing over of money, of course, is a righteous act in itself, but there is also a tradition of making anonymous donations of cash to a person in need with no expectation that the money will be returned. The hope is that the good deed will be contagious and lead the recipients, when they're back on their feet again, to help someone else out. But one of the highest forms of charity in Jewish thinking is to give a person a job to enable them to support themselves without relying on others. In practice you will find that becoming a Jew will involve you in all sorts of charitable work where you'll be expected to pledge money or, just as important, time to charitable causes within the community.

Charity in Christian thought is associated with love – love of one's fellow human beings, love of God, and a reciprocation of God's love for you. It also carries with it an element of self-sacrifice; not just giving cash because you have money to spare but giving money you can ill-afford to spend. If you're contemplating a Christian lifestyle you will be made familiar, pretty early on, with Jesus' Parable of the Widow's Mite. Though her donation to the Temple coffers was insignificant (two mites, the smallest denomination amounting to a mere farthing), Jesus judged her to have given far more than anyone else. The rich who had made large donations could easily afford to do so; the widow was effectively giving everything she had. So the moral is clear – and not a little disconcerting – if you're preparing to take the Christian road: the more you have the more you'll be expected to give.

In Islam, charitable giving is enshrined in the Prophet's teaching and in two principles – *zakah* and *sadaqah*. The first is so central to the faith that it is considered one of the five 'Pillars of Islam'. It translates broadly as a religious tax that is expected of every practising Muslim and which is used, in the service of Allah, for the collective good. Muslims are expected to provide for their families and dependants first but of the surplus remaining they are also expected to donate one-fortieth to help the poor and the needy. As you'll have seen, the maths has already been done for you. Expect to have to contribute something like 2.5 per cent of your disposable income – not counting what you offer as *sadaqah*, or charitable donations, in response to unpredictable need such as famines, droughts and similar natural disasters.

As a Buddhist you will be expected to follow the principle of *dana*, or generosity in giving (particularly to monks, nuns, and other spiritually developed people). This is considered a specifically religious act and is said to purify the mind of the giver and help in the process of enlightenment. Acquisition of and attachment to things contribute towards further suffering in the world so by giving and thereby freeing yourself from such negative impulses you gain merit in the world. Though reward for your generosity is not what you seek, you will nonetheless be blessed. Paradoxically, the more you give away the wealthier you will become in mind and body.

As a Hindu you will similarly be expected to make a devotional offering, or *bhiksha*, which it's believed will bring you specific rewards in this and subsequent lives. Giving food, for example, according to the mythological Hindu sage Vasistha, will reward you with beautiful eyes and a good memory while giving an umbrella will theoretically bring you a house in return. As in Judaism, anonymous giving is particularly virtuous and is said to free you from your sins and open up the doors of heaven.

By becoming a Jain you would be entering into a marvellously paradoxical community. You will be joining people who live the simplest of lives – non-smoking, non-drinking vegetarians – but whose hard work has made them one of the wealthiest classes in India with a long and generous record of charitable giving to some of the subcontinent's most prestigious institutions. Internal factionalism has weakened the united front the religion traditionally showed to the world and there are those who say it has become less welcoming to newcomers but Jainism at its best is still a glowing example of selfless service to humanity. Its monks and nuns embody that spirit in their everyday lives, wandering possession-less – some entirely naked – across the Earth in pursuit of holiness. You won't necessarily have to strip off and join them but their example will be an inspiration.

The tithing practised commonly by Jews and Christians is also carried out by Sikhs where the concept of *dasvand* (literally 'a tenth part') applies. As with other religions, you're going to have to tot up the cost of becoming a Sikh and weigh it against the benefits, which, to be fair, are considerable. You will be joining an immensely sociable grouping with a real commitment to both their own and to wider society. Putting back a tenth of your income into such a supportive community is cheap at the price.

Business life

By common consent modern China is enjoying an economic boom and it is interesting to note how, in this most money-driven of societies, an ancient philosophy is making a comeback. Policy-makers and company bigwigs have noticed how the 2,500-year-old tradition of Confucianism is beginning to give twentieth-century Marxist ideology a run for its money. Perhaps you'd like to join it, too.

You'll need to have a strong sense of order and routine, discipline and respect, and to value hierarchies in political, social and business life. The concept of filial piety will ensure you don't give your parents any backchat and listen carefully to what they have to say. You'll study hard, be obedient to your teachers and be aware of the difference between right and wrong. Creating a harmonious society and avoiding social unrest will be among your goals, as will respecting your elders and those in senior levels of management above you. There's evidence that there's a huge market for this sort of approach.

In 2006 the Beijing University Professor Yu Dan appeared on state TV to explain the classic of Confucianism, *The Analects*, in plain language. Following it up with a short book on the subject, she went on to sell over 4 million copies – double, according to a *Washington Post* report, the sales volume of the previous bestseller, *Harry Potter and the Philosopher's Stone*. Although some criticized its selective and, they claimed, distorted view of the philosophy, there's clearly an appetite for it.

On the other hand, China also seems to be rediscovering the values of Taoism in its economic life. The business mogul and Taoist patron Zhu Tieyu, for example, attributes his financial success to the principles of his religion. Once a small-time hustler devoted to ducking, diving and making money where he could, he says the religion turned his life around. Ironically, it was, he says, the very non-competitiveness of Taoism that allowed him to rise to the top of the very competitive business world. The principle of *wu wei*, active inaction, of going with the flow of life rather than against the grain, taught him patience and discipline. Taking his cue from nature, developing his breathing exercises and, above all, channelling the *ch'i*, or vital energy of the universe, allowed him to follow his instincts and patiently bide his time before seizing business opportunities that have made him a wealthy man.

In the same way, Jewish, Christian, Muslim, Sikh, Buddhist and Hindu business people will tell you they owe their success not only to hard work, thrift and intelligence but to codes of business ethics that embody mutual and collective responsibilities.

The Talmud, the codification of Jewish law, for example, muses on the type of questions that might be asked of you by God after your death and concludes that one of them will be 'Did you conduct your business affairs with honesty and probity?' Jewish business ethics takes into account not only relationships with employees, customers, and the wider society but proper relationships with *competitors*. It is not enough to make money at all costs. It has to be done fairly, with honesty and without lying. That's why the Bernie Madoff affair exploded like a bombshell within the American Jewish community. Sure, it was a question of money – big money – but it was principally a question of ethics, of right Jewish conduct. Madoff may yet be rehabilitated (the rabbis would say 'redeemed'), but, boy, does he have a lot to make up for, namely ignoring an ethical code of behaviour in public life that has lasted over three millennia is no small crime.

Likewise, Islamic law has its own code of business ethics, listing the duties of employees and employers alike to act honourably. The employee is charged with giving his or her employer a day's work for a day's pay, not wasting time or being lazy. In return, the employer has to look after the general well-being of the workforce above all, paying staff fairly and without delay. 'Give the worker his wages before his sweat dries,' comments one Islamic source. But these ethics are binding not just on business people but on customers, too. So, if you're taking the Jewish or Islamic option, don't go into a camera shop, say, spend an hour being shown the options, and then go and buy the camera you've chosen for less online. That's wasting time and, essentially, being dishonest. Becoming a religious person means curbing your selfish impulses and thinking about the mutual good of all.

However, what religious business people will tell you is that ethical business pays. It is successful – it makes money and, in turn, spreads the wealth around. One wise Sikh professional man who runs a profitable business in the Midlands but who spends all his available spare time doing community work from the local gurdwara told me that his prayers now contain the plea, 'Lord, please don't let me make any *more* money. I have enough.'

The communal life

You may, of course, wish to turn your back on the sharp-elbowed hurly-burly of the business world and retreat into a more contemplative world where collaboration rather than competition is the watchword. You'll have no shortage of options to choose from. The communal life features prominently in many faiths.

It flourishes principally in the monastic traditions of both east and west, where the Roman Catholic Church established, a vow of poverty, alongside vows of chastity and obedience. Each prospective monk or nun renounces worldly goods and retreats into a world where matters of the spirit predominate. The great paradox, of course, is that, while they have nothing, they have everything. Not for them worries about mortgages, paying the bills, knowing where the next penny is going to come from. Instead, they are given money according to need. Food and clothing, heating and lighting, plus a (fairly) comfortable bed and a modest room, are all provided. The rest, money to visit a relative or to make a trip outside the monastery grounds, has to be requested and will be granted at the discretion of the abbot or mother superior. Every monk and nun I've ever met thrives on it. They're youthful in outlook, full of energy for the most part and, considering themselves rich in all things, thoroughly content. The would-be convert to this lifestyle will soon realize that, when you have nothing, you have nothing to lose. It's a liberating prospect to consider for those of us weighed down with the sheer burden of possessions.

At the extreme end of the scale, you might consider becoming a 'sky-clad' Jain monk. You certainly won't need money – not least because you'll have nowhere to put it – and you'll be forced to rely on other people's charity for your survival. The life of the mendicant Buddhist monk or Hindu holy man is similarly devoid of those physical attachments to the world that can so overwhelm an ordinary person in the material, consumerist west. About the only thing a Zen Buddhist monk in Seoul has to call his own, for example, is his rice bowl. But is his life really any the poorer for it?

Judaism has never embraced the ascetic life and so privation/liberation of this order is not part of the Jewish experience. Collectivity and mutuality, however, are – but take place within the context of the home, the family and the synagogue. It is no accident that nineteenth-century Anglican Christian reformers and their heirs within the Methodist Church were a powerful driving force behind the cooperative movement, which promotes shared ownership and business run not primarily for profit but for the mutual benefit and welfare of its members. Of course, you don't have to be religious to back such a movement (as we know, Karl Marx, who lent his name to a cooperative ideology of his own, was not himself taken with religion, branding it 'the opium of the people'). However, to leave religious reformers out of the picture gives only a partial view of collective enterprise.

You could also consider the communal life of Mennonite and Amish sects but, if you do, be prepared to turn your back on many of the consumer luxuries you've probably been used to up until now. No phones, tellies, radios, baseball games, iPods or CDs. No cars to take you far away from the community (and, crucially to bring in outsiders who might threaten it). In short, a life of frugality and moderation, earning what is necessary to support a family and a community. There's a lot worse you could do, let's face it.

Some experiments in communal living do go wrong – usually because of the strong personality of a charismatic leader who finds himself (usually a 'he', it has to be said) acting in an increasingly autocratic way. Jim Jones in Guyana, David Koresh at Waco, the Bhagwan Shree Rajneesh in Oregon all presided over communes that collapsed amid allegations of mind control and abuse of power. More mainstream Christian communities have also crashed and burned. Becoming part of an established religious group is no guarantee of success. Those who have studied these collective movements (at their best, liberating places that allow potential to flourish and, at their worst, destructive cults that exploit and enslave) urge potential recruits to study the small print carefully – in particular finding out in advance how easy it is going to be to leave if you find out the lifestyle is not to your taste after all.

Should religious people be wealthy?

The Christian gospels are full of opinions on the relative merits of wealth and poverty but Jesus himself implied that there were particular dangers associated with wealth. Selling all you have and giving to the poor in order to acquire treasures in heaven (Matthew 19:21) seems pretty clear. Likewise Jesus' comments two verses later in which he compares getting into heaven with Peter Kay getting into a pair of Speedos (author's paraphrase) suggest that wealth is a serious bar to godliness.

That said, what is one to make of the Vatican – simultaneously the rock on which Jesus Christ built his Church and the repository of incalculable temporal riches in the form of priceless artistic treasures, land and real estate? What of the American mega-churches with a charitable income equal to the GDP of a small African state? What is one to make of the caliphs and emirs who commissioned vast mosques inlaid with gold, silver, and lapis lazuli instead of distributing that accumulated wealth to the needy children of Almighty Allah? Religion's detractors would call it a clear case of hypocrisy and the kind of double standard that could be dreamed up only by a club of holy Joes having their celestial cake and eating it. And yet …

Consider the New Testament account of the woman with the jar of expensive perfume (Matthew 26:7) who disturbed the disciples' supper in order to anoint Jesus' head only to be told, sanctimoniously, that she could have put the perfume to better use by selling it and giving the proceeds to the poor. Now it is Jesus of all people who defends the extravagance (where are Peter Kay's trunks and the needle's eye when you need them?). And it is Jesus who, in the process, turns financial pragmatism on its head.

There are many ways to make money and many ways to spend it. If you want quick ways to make it, some Christian preachers will tell you to subscribe to their brand of 'prosperity theology' whereby, if you truly believe, you will be granted the wealth you desire. Maybe you will. Or maybe you'll blame yourself for being a timid believer if you don't. Maybe you'll get the same thing if you join Buddhism's largest lay group, Soka Gakkai, and chant the Lotus Sutra in expectation of your heart's desire. Maybe you'll get it if you become a Wiccan and turn your wallet three times by the light of the crescent moon to draw money towards you. Maybe you'll get it if you study the neo-Confucian *I Ching*, or Book of Changes, one of the Thirteen Classics of Chinese thought and culture. Who knows?

And if you make your wealth, then what? How are you going to spend it? Well, that, of course, is where the religious texts leave off and your personal conscience kicks in. Money, you'll remember, is not the root of all evil. Love of it is.

★
★★
★

TOP THREE

1 A tie between **Judaism, Islam, Sikhism** and **Hinduism** for their community solidarity and the realization that, as minority faiths, they have no one to fall back on but themselves. There are no automatic state handouts, only the sacrificial giving of their members to guarantee their survival.

NEAR MISS

The Digambara sect of **Jainism**. Giving up everything including your clothes takes real commitment. Respect!

11

Recreation

Let the good times roll

Two of the most common complaints voiced by young (and not so young) non-religious people in the west are that religion is boring and that the practice of faith is incompatible with having a good time. Their use of the word 'good' is instructive because those who contest this twin assertion would argue that having a good time is exactly what religion is all about. Both sides have a point.

All too often goodness can seem less attractive than dangerous and edgy non-conformity. In life, look how many women are attracted to the rogues and the bad lads rather than to the nice, dependable boy next door. In literature, look how Milton's Satan is by far the most interesting and attractive character of *Paradise Lost*. And, in music, how we know instinctively that the Devil has all the best tunes. The 'Goodfellas' of Martin Scorsese's mafia classic of the same name are anything but good. And yet their allure is irresistible and the girls can't help themselves. As any writer will tell you, making goodness interesting is a difficult trick to pull off.

But the religions beg to differ. Jews have a sacred duty to enjoy life and on the Day of Judgement will be asked to account for all the legitimate pleasures they denied themselves on Earth. Christians are told that Jesus came so that we should all have life more abundantly. Muslims consider the ultimate pleasure to be obeying Allah's will. And Buddhists know that enlightenment lies beyond the transitory illusions of this world.

So can the two sides ever see eye to eye? Is it possible to pick a religion that doesn't seem to be regimenting or restricting your free time – one that, in short, isn't preventing you from enjoying yourself?

The simple answer is yes. Or they'd have all gone out of business long ago. But – and there's always a but – it will take some readjustment and a different perspective on the entire pleasure principle before you can appreciate the different sorts of satisfaction the religions provide. So there's a cost–benefit analysis to be carried out and you alone must decide what things you are prepared to sacrifice in order to enjoy the benefits of whatever choice you make.

Nights in White City

If the turnover from the drinks industry is anything to go by (£36.6 billion in the UK alone according to 2004 figures from the Department for Food, Environment and Rural Affairs) a visitor from Mars would be forgiven for concluding that the country's entire recreational activity revolves around alcohol. It doesn't need me to paint a pen portrait of the human wreckage on the streets of our towns and cities any night of the week after 11 p.m. From Guildford to Grimsby, from Whitehaven to White City, it's alcoholic mayhem out there. We've all seen it, even perhaps once been part of it.

But say goodbye to all that if you want to go down the religion route. A night on the lash is simply not an option for most if not all of the adherents of the world faiths. Islam, Hinduism, Sikhism, Buddhism, Jainism, Taoism, Rastafarianism and Mormonism specifically forbid the consumption of alcohol. The Baha'is, the Amish, the Mennonites, the Methodists (mostly), and Seventh Day Adventists never touch it and of those adherents that do (Zoroastrians, Christians (Christ's first recorded miracle, remember, was turning water into wine), Jews, Neopagans, Shintoists and followers of Candomblé, Voodoo and the Native indigenous religions) none would condone random drinking to excess. There are limited occasions when inebriation is encouraged for religious reasons (more anon) but the general rule is that drunkenness and lack of self-control are way offside.

You're probably also likely to have to steer pretty clear of the pub, bar and club scene – partly, of course, because of the alcohol but also because of the general air of immodesty and excess that surrounds many of these establishments in Britain today. Going down the pub in any case is a cultural event more associated with northern climes (think of the Norse god Odin who is said to have lived off nothing but wine and beer). It's simply not something your average Jew, Muslim, Sikh or Hindu would *want* to do – even if keeping 'religiously' to orange juice and sparkling water all night.

There is one time of the year, however, when Orthodox Jews are religiously enjoined to have one (or several) over the eight. This is on the festival of Purim commemorating the deliverance of the Jews from exile in the Persian Empire and recorded in the book of Esther (the only book of the Bible, incidentally, not to mention the word God). On this festive day amid much merrymaking (and dressing up for the children) Jewish men are encouraged to get so hammered that they are unable to distinguish the name of their historical oppressor from that of their deliverer. Needless to say, some rabbis have suggested toning this down a bit and understanding the instruction metaphorically (having one glass more than usual, say, followed by a befuddled snooze). Either way, however, drink is taken in copious quantities as a religious obligation. If you like a drop of the hard stuff and aren't averse to pushing the boat out once in a while, this could be for you. Only once a year, mind, and think of your head the next morning. Moderation in all things, you could say, including moderation.

Espresso bongo

So what about an hour with friends over tea or coffee? 'Fraid not if you're planning to become a Rastafarian, a Seventh Day Adventist, or a Mormon, who are all forbidden from taking stimulants of which caffeine is one.

Smoking is not actively encouraged in any religion (apart from marijuana in Rastafarianism, which extols it, under controlled circumstances, as the 'herb of healing and the weed of wisdom'). Most religions these days recognize the health risks and advise against it. The Islamic view of smoking neatly sums up the general religious approach to tobacco. There are five categories of action: what Allah has decreed, what Allah has forbidden, what Allah has recommended but not insisted on, what Allah has disapproved of but not expressly forbidden, and what Allah has remained silent about. Smoking appears to be in that grey area somewhere in the middle. And certainly in North Africa, the Mediterranean, and the Middle East smoking seems to be a national pastime among Muslim men.

Christianity is similarly undecided about banning smoking altogether. Texts comparing the body to a temple and injunctions not to defile it are quoted at length, but the reality remains that many Christians do smoke (including, by the way, a surprising number of Catholic priests). The ban on smoking in public buildings in Britain, however, and the increasing social disapproval of smoking at all means that fewer and fewer Christians are likely to take up the habit in the first place.

If you're inclined to have an occasional flutter on the horses, many religions, likewise, will broadly disapprove – not always for the gambling itself but for the peripheral lifestyle of dissolution and irresponsibility with which it is associated. Afghanistan's Taliban even went so far as to ban chess on the grounds that they believed it to be a form of gambling. Mind you, they also banned kite flying and bird keeping for being un-Islamic so there's no accounting for what some religions will accept and some forbid.

Perhaps because of its Irish connections and Ireland's attachment to horse racing, the Catholic Church has never come down too heavily on gambling unless, of course, it gets out of control and becomes an addiction threatening individuals and families. Chinese cultures, however, have often actively encouraged it, believing that good luck is a blessing from the Gods.

Those tempted to risk a few quid on the 2.45 at Kempton Park could do well to study the *I Ching*, or Book of Changes, one of the ancient Chinese classics outlining a system of divination too complex to describe here. By casting bones or shells or stones and reading off their patterns against a table of correspondences it's thought that the practitioner can gain some insight into the future. Confucianism, Taoism and Chinese folk religion could well be for you, then, if your idea of recreation is spending an hour with the *Racing Post* trying to pick winners.

Love is in the air

If alcohol is one of the West's major reasons for going out in the evening, so, too, is the prospect of meeting members of the opposite sex. If you're a married person reading this then what follows will be irrelevant. If you're single and don't want to be for much longer it could be significant.

Signing up to most of the world religions means that your opportunity to mix with the opposite sex will be severely curtailed. This may not be a bad thing – as will be explained in a moment – but it will mean a radical departure from what you have probably been used to so far. The chances are that, as a non-religious person born and brought up in Britain, you'll have been accustomed to an atmosphere where the free intermingling of the sexes has been taken as read. You probably went to a mixed school, may have gone to university, are perhaps working in an office, factory or shop – all places where the sexes mix as a matter of course. It will have been natural, therefore, to want to mix in the same way over a drink after lectures or work.

Not any more. At least if you're thinking of opting into certain groupings of Judaism, Islam, Sikhism and Hinduism where random encounters with the opposite sex are frequently viewed with suspicion. The idea of flirting or dating is frowned on in these traditional societies where young women in particular are restricted as to where (and with whom) they might venture once they have left the house.

Broadly speaking, the extended family with its network of uncles, aunts, nephews, nieces, cousins and close friends is the expected arena for forming relationships. Inevitably, in modern Britain men and women from all religions and none mix more freely than in the past, but conservative-minded communities want to oversee and to some extent choreograph relationships between the sexes. Arranged marriages are the norm and the idea that a couple will go out with each other for a few months having met at a party, decide they've had enough of each other, part and start all over again with a new partner is out of the question. Indeed, the whole notion of a 'party' in traditional Jewish, Islamic or eastern religious cultures is far different from what a secular westerner would have in mind.

The nearest event to a party would be a wedding or birthday celebration when interaction between the sexes would be highly controlled. Dancing, for example, has sensual connotations that make it beyond the pale for most of these communities. Where there is dancing it is a single-sex affair shorn of any sexual intent. There is something extraordinarily touching in the sight of an elderly Hasidic Jew in his fur hat and silk tunic taking to the floor to the accompaniment of a vibrant klezmer band and taking hold of his friends' hands without the slightest sense of embarrassment or surprise before throwing himself into a dance. Likewise, Sikh and Hindu girls, dressed in their finest outfits to enjoy a wedding reception, dance with each other. Of course, they make sure the boys see them arriving and taking to the dance floor, but it would be out of the question for a boy and girl to dance closely together.

All the religions at some point in their history have been suspicious of popular dancing. Aside from liturgical dance designed as an adjunct of worship, the association of bodily movement with the promotion of sexual desire has been inescapable. This has sometimes provoked an extreme and arguably hysterical reaction out of all proportion to an activity, which, as morris dancing clearly proves, need not always be sensually charged. It's also provoked a slew of off-colour jokes along the lines of 'Question: why do Scottish Calvinists not permit sex standing up? Answer: because from a distance it might look like you're dancing.' Boom boom. Vulgar but very funny – and not far from the truth. For Scottish Calvinists, by the way, you can substitute many another religious group.

Some conservative sects aside, contemporary western Christianity is probably the most liberal in its acceptance of the mixing of the sexes. Those who have attended Christian youth clubs in the hope of meeting the opposite sex will be familiar with the chaste (but often highly charged) atmosphere surrounding these encounters round the pool table or on the badminton court, the whole event supervised and chaperoned by a kindly young minister and his wife. Things have changed over the years and no one raises an eyebrow at boys and girls mixing and even holding hands. And it's true that, despite such an accepting (other religions might say dangerously liberal) approach, the sky hasn't fallen in nor the world come to an end. Perhaps it is only a matter of time before some of the religions take note and follow suit. But, in picking the religion appropriate for you, don't expect that to happen overnight.

Making your own amusement

If you're attached to such forms of entertainment as the TV, radio, cinema, theatre and so on, you may find that some conservative religious groups disapprove. Indeed, many Orthodox Jews, traditionalist Muslims and conservative Christians would have a problem with the very notion of entertainment in the first place. Entertainment, they would argue, is essentially a distraction from the religious things that endure. Reading fiction or magazines, watching TV or listening to radio have all, in their time, been branded un-Christian, un-Islamic, or against the tenets of the Jewish faith. But there's a wide divergence of opinion even within those religions as to what is or isn't acceptable. So make enquiries before you commit yourself.

Should you be considering Judaism as an option, you will soon be introduced to the uniqueness of the Sabbath, when recreation is made an obligatory part of the week. From the Friday night meal to sunset on Saturday no work is done and time is spent in worship, study or deepening family relationships over meals, conversation, walks in the park or whatever. Husbands and wives, you may remember, are encouraged to have physical relations on the Sabbath in celebration of this day of rest. There'll be a hundred and one things you *can't* do, of course, from switching on your computer to driving down to the coast, but what you are allowed to do will recharge your batteries like nothing else. Not for nothing is the day set aside for *re*-creation, making yourself and the world anew.

Sabbath observance among Christians is not as strict as it once was. In Calvinist, Pentecostal, Presbyterian, Methodist and Evangelical households until quite recently churchgoing twice or even three times on Sunday was not uncommon. Nowadays you'll mostly find it's limited to once and you'll have a choice between morning and evening worship – home in time to switch the TV on to watch *Songs of Praise* if you feel like it.

What counts as recreation in a Bruderhof or Amish household is quite different. Here pastimes are simple – a spot of carpentry, some fishing, or that quintessentially female pursuit, the sewing of a 'love quilt'. Half a dozen or more women gather round a table sewing their portion of a quilt, all the while talking (not gossiping, which is strictly forbidden) about things happening in the community. It's a unique institution that can bond, heal, comfort, provoke and uplift. Now that's entertainment.

Sport as recreation poses a problem for some communities. Many Muslims and Jews worry not only about the gender interaction but often about the supposed immodesty of sporting gear. As a budding female (and Orthodox Jewish) ice-skater, for example, you'll probably be expected to wear a long dress rather than a short one … if you're allowed to go to the rink at all. As someone from a devout Muslim household you may not be allowed to go swimming or play badminton unless properly conforming to the Islamic dress code.

Compromises are inevitable, however – particularly in western societies where outside secular influences are impossible to avoid. Theoretically, the boxer Danny Williams, a devout Muslim, knew he shouldn't really be a fighter because of what the Koran says about laying a fist on another's face. But equally he is a superb sportsman with what he and his understanding community know to be a God-given gift. As a result, his fellow Muslims discreetly turned a blind eye to what the Book said in one text and turned to another to justify his career. Compromise number one. Compromise number two was eventually to retire from the ring – but only after he had become heavyweight champion.

The trade-off for accepting such religious restrictions, however, is that you get to enjoy a close family and community life. Sometimes, of course, this can be too close and too restricting – particularly, in traditional families, for women. In the west, there will be some scope for negotiation but be prepared for a lifestyle shock – though not always an unpleasant one.

Let's end this section with a story told to me by a liberal Catholic friend of mine who several years ago had secured rare access to one such traditional Amish family in Pennsylvania in order to make a documentary. At first he found the restrictions hard to take. No electric light, no radio, no TV, no music, no cars, none of the mod cons he'd been used to and an altogether austere life that seemed distinctly short on pleasure.

Yet he was profoundly aware of a real sense of community, with strong family affection and genuine interaction between all the ages. One evening, returning from an interview in town, he found himself alone with time on his hands and decided to drop into a bar for a welcome beer. He lit a cigar, sat down to enjoy the beer then, amid the noise and the smoky atmosphere of the saloon, realized that he was missing the simplicity, order and – yes – *wholesomeness* of the Amish lifestyle. The cigar soon lost its savour and the beer its attraction, so he took his leave without finishing either.

What he had thought of as recreation had become a wearisome chore and what he thought lacked all excitement and stimulation was where the real and lasting pleasure lay. Choose your religion wisely and you'll be able to share a comparable experience for yourself.

1 **Liberal Christianity** for having largely accepted most forms of entertainment as neutral in themselves. It allows a large measure of freedom to all its members to follow the lifestyle that suits them and has accepted that the Church has to function in the context of society as a whole with all its temptations. It's aware of the real temptations of the modern world but is doing its best to offer an equally real and attractive alternative.

2 Progressive **Judaism** for its strong sense of family and community but also for its acceptance that young people in particular cannot be forced to enjoy such values. The faith has to be made attractive enough for people to want to stay within the community and discover their real pleasure there.

3 **Sikhism** for its family values but also for its ability to integrate into mainstream society and play a full part in it. It allows its members the freedom to mix socially and in the context of work but offers a fulfilling community life where people feel they really belong.

12

Worship and contemplation

The way of the kami

Prepare to enter a sacred space. You begin by stepping through the wooden archway at the end of the tree-lined lane and, as you do so, you exchange one world for another. Soon you realize you have left behind the everyday world of noises and distractions and have arrived at a place of peace and calm. You are moving into the abode of the *kami*, the spirits who reside in the natural landscape, and this is their shrine. Welcome to the world of Shinto, the ancient indigenous religion of Japan.

At the entrance to the shrine is a trough of water where you wash your hands in an act of ritual purification. Next you move to the prayer hall where the *kami* will be alerted to your presence by the sound of two hand claps. After bowing deeply and placing a monetary offering in a collection box, you proceed to your devotions and your prayers can begin. If your taste is for ritual and formality in worship, then Shinto offers you both.

You write your prayer requests on a small wooden board and hang it on the wall alongside hundreds of others. In time they will be ceremonially burned by the Shinto priest in an annual offering to the spirits who will in their own time consider your appeals. There are no restrictions on what you can pray for and many will unashamedly ask for personal rewards and favours – winning the lottery, for example, of giving up smoking. If instant gratification is what you search (or at least the promise of it) Shinto will oblige. Unlike other religions, which tacitly require you to pray for such tiresome things as fortitude, patience, wisdom or understanding (qualities less definable than a new car or a promotion at work), Shinto allows you to ask for what you wish. And who knows, the *kami* might oblige.

The downside to all this, however, is that they might not and, when angered or offended, might strike back without warning. The Japanese earthquake and tsunami of 2011 were seen by many as an example of just such an impulse and there was no shortage of people questioning the wisdom of siting nuclear reactors on those stretches of the natural landscape (geological fault lines, for example) that would offend the native spirits of place. Look at Hokusai's famous woodblock print of *The Great Wave off Kanagawa* if you want to see how artists have imagined the consequences of such divine retribution – and notice how the humans in that seascape are prostrate in terror at nature's fury as the sacred Mount Fuji in the background looks impassively on.

And rest assured that, if you do adopt Shinto as your chosen religion, you will never look at the natural world in the same way again. Instead, your worship will be driven by the knowledge that there are unseen forces everywhere ready to repay you in kind. For good measure, you might also like to acquire a protective amulet to carry with you or place on a *kami* shelf at home. You can never be too careful.

Circles, groves and magic potions

If this appeal to the Earth and to the forces within it attracts you, you have a number of other spiritual options at hand.

Druidry, for instance, whose modern-day origins stretch back a couple of hundred years, is a nature-based religion you might like to consider. Don't worry, you won't be expected to indulge in animal sacrifice (the ancient Celts may have done so at one time but nowadays any offerings are of flowers or incense and certainly not of blood). The Druid Network and the grandly titled Order of Bards, Ovates and Druids will keep you in touch with all the year's major festivals that even city dwellers in high-rise flats can celebrate to remind them of their proximity to and reverence for Mother Earth.

Sacred groves, wells, glades and glens are the ideal spots for Druid worship – though admittedly these are in short supply in north London or central Manchester. Nonetheless, worship can take place anywhere, prompted as much by seasonal milestones such as the winter solstice or the coming of spring as by tangible sites in the physical landscape. Satisfying the twin attractions of time and place is the annual trek to Stonehenge where, within this sacred circle, rituals to greet the midsummer sun are performed amid (and often dwarfed by) crowds that would rival those on Oxford Street on Boxing Day. It is easy to be snooty about this mass invasion of New Age day-trippers. But it is testimony to the mysterious power of Stonehenge that, even in the twenty-first century CE, it still continues to attract the kind of awestruck pilgrim it did in the early Bronze Age.

In addition to the summer solstice, you can add to your adopted Druid calendar of events such festivals as Imbolc to mark the coming of spring, Beltane, or Mayday, the harvest festival of Lughnasadh, and the traditional Celtic new year, Samhain. Until recently the Druid Network held its annual Lammas Games in August on a field in rural Oxfordshire and there a small gathering of Druids and their families would camp out for a few days, singing songs, playing games and eating together – just as their distant ancestors had done thousands of years ago in celebration of the harvest being safely gathered in. It was a lively, fun event (and now much-missed) in which, dear reader, I myself had the privilege of 'competing' some years ago, writing myself a minor footnote in Druid history by coming an ignominious last in the 'wife carrying' race. This was not reported widely in the sports pages of the national press.

Such is the attachment to the sacred ancestral land that Australian Aborigine and Native American and African spiritual religions are largely confined to their respective continents, but occasionally even in cities small expatriate communities gather to perform their rituals. I well remember taking part in an impromptu invocation of the Yoruba god of iron, Ogun, a major deity of the Yoruba people of West Africa. Fortified by whisky the celebrant intoned prayers to summon the spirit of the celestial blacksmith into our presence, welcomed with offerings of bitter kola nuts. And where was this garden? In Benin, Togo or Nigeria? No. It was attached to a small terraced house off Ladbroke Grove in west London and appeared to sway (was it the scotch?) to the strains of the American jazz saxophonist John Coltrane, himself taken to be a god worthy of joining the African pantheon.

Of course, those drawn to the practices of Haitian Voodoo will be familiar with the easy mixing of deities drawn from a variety of spiritual sources (theologians call it syncretism). Ogun (and even John Coltrane) have found themselves co-opted at various times as *orishas*, or supernatural spirits, who have taken their place alongside traditional Roman Catholic saints in that unique fusion of religions known as Voodoo, Santería or Candomblé. The media have not by and large served these traditions well, associating them in popular culture with devil worship, human sacrifice and that staple of B movie horror, the zombie. In practice, they are, for the most part, folk beliefs that sit naturally (if sometimes controversially) within mainstream Catholic worship and which provide identity and belonging for the people, especially the poor, from Haiti to New Orleans.

The Voodoo doll is perhaps the best-known and most misunderstood item in the practitioner's spiritual toolkit. Its attraction lies in its supposed power, and perhaps you, too, might like to share it. Just as spells and magic potions will, it's believed, remove evil spirits and bad luck so the doll will control, it's hoped, the bodily functions of the person it's constructed to represent. Most hope that it will cure or rejuvenate the person in question and are drawn to its imagined powers for pure motives. Others, however, of a more malevolent turn of mind may wish ill on people (think pins, scary music, and ham acting at the movies). But remember that superstition has, at its root, fear and that magic is predicated on power. So you would be well advised to mull over the implications of constructing an effigy of your love rival or business competitor just in case that fear were to transfer itself to you and that power suddenly become too much to control.

Altered states

The addition of a little rum at Voodoo ceremonies does more than make the evening go with a swing. Artificial stimulants have a long pedigree in religious ritual but are to be treated with caution.

As part of their worshipping rituals Rastafarians traditionally use *ganja*, or marijuana, to heighten their sense of communion with God, or Jah. This 'herb of healing and weed of wisdom' is often an integral (and, in Britain, illegal) part of the process of divining the truth of existence at the so-called 'reasoning sessions' where such theology is discussed. In using such a drug they thus join a line of users stretching from the ancient Israelites to some modern Hindu and Sufi Muslim sects. It may just be worth explaining that to the arresting officers as you are invited to take a seat in the back of their van.

Whatever the supposed spiritual benefits, however, it would be foolish for would-be practitioners of any of these religious traditions to ignore the risks to mental health associated with long-term use. There are reports of shamans, witch doctors, and medicine men of the American Indian traditions driven to madness and death in their attempts to travel through the spirit world and return safely to their earthbound lives. The use of mind-altering drugs such as the cactus derivative, peyote, or the many species of hallucinatory mushrooms is surely not to be left out of the equation when explaining such instances of mental fragility.

Shamanism, increasingly popular in the west, is best considered only by experienced and trained practitioners of sound mental state. The idea is for shamans to free themselves of this earthly realm and to travel along some astral plane encountering spirits along the way. As in ancient Egyptian lore, some of these spirits will be benevolent and some mischievous and malicious. The shaman's job is to meet them (in some cases defeat them) and to bring back insights that will help the living. Being stranded in such a spirit world is distinctly unwise and stories suggest dire consequences for those who bungle the task – comparable perhaps to the reported psychotic after-effects of some mind-altering substances. All of which makes a nip of rum at a Voodoo séance sound like a sip of communion wine at a Church of England service.

Peace at last

At the opposite end of the spectrum from the intensely physical experiences of the shaman is the quiet meditation of the Buddhist. Those of you who've had a gentle introduction to Buddhism through the practice of yoga may be ready to take things a little further and to develop those mental attitudes leading to enlightenment. But bear in mind that this development will not happen overnight. Immediate gratification is not the Buddhist way and it will take weeks, months, years of training the mind through discipline and dedication. Only then will you be free of the illusions of this world and able to appreciate your and the world's true nature.

For this you will need to appreciate the Four Noble Truths: that all human experience is suffering; that craving for permanence in this world is the cause of suffering; that suffering can be ended, and that nirvana, or true enlightenment, and the end of all suffering are possible through the Eightfold Path. Of the qualities you as a practitioner will need to develop along this path, right knowledge and right attitude can be listed under the heading of wisdom and understanding; right speech, right action and right livelihood under the heading of moral and ethical behaviour; and right effort, right mindfulness and right concentration under the heading of mental discipline.

Meditation can begin with something as simple as the breath, hearing its rhythms and perhaps thinking of a single word such as 'peace', 'stillness', or 'love' (or that heartbeat of Creation, the mystical syllable Om, or Aum) on every slow exhalation. It may involve gazing on a picture or a flower and being thoroughly attentive to the moment. Teachers will help you develop these skills (and reading the texts will help complement them) but cultivating stillness on your own is a start. Choose a warm quiet spot where you will not be disturbed and off you go.

Of course you will have different movements and schools to choose from: the ancient Theravada Buddhism of Thailand, Laos, Burma, Sri Lanka and Cambodia or the Mahayana tradition with its various schools that emerged in China, Tibet, Mongolia, Vietnam, Korea and Japan. But it is in those moments of meditation and silent contemplation that your journey will begin. A perfect antidote to the stresses and tensions of metropolitan life and a proven way of lowering your blood pressure and saying goodbye to road rage for good.

The Venerable Hyon Gak Sunim (b. 1964), Zen Buddhist teacher at the 500-year-old Hwa Gye Sah Temple in Seoul, South Korea.

(Born Paul Muenzen to a family of devout Catholics in New Jersey, Hyon Gak Sunim was the first westerner to be ordained a Buddhist monk in China since the Cultural Revolution.)

The temple schedule generally starts at 3 a.m. Some monks get up earlier. We start with chanting and meditation, looking inside and studying the question, 'What am I?'. We're not hermits, we do go out into the community caring for the sick and the destitute and performing Buddhist ceremonies where they are wanted. What I do is very similar to the work of a parish priest but it doesn't show up on the radar in that way. **Buddhism isn't evangelical.** *It's like the groundwater under the earth; you never see it, you never hear it but it's there. And when it disappears people die.*

As a westerner I'm an oddity. I get stuff on the street like, 'Heh, you come from America. You should be Christian,' and I laugh. I can't say it was like winning the lottery for my family when I became a Buddhist. They're devout Catholic believers and couldn't understand it. But they were patient and now my mother says I'm a better Christian than my eight brothers and sisters. They're city bankers earning tons of cash but she looks at them and sees they're always fearful of losing their job or whatever and she looks at me and sees that **I'm content just as I am.**

*We have to **live** in the moment. To hear the sound of the wind, to really hear it, that's enlightenment. To taste the taste of a pickle, to feel the wind on your face in the moment, to be in tune with what you're doing NOW – there's nothing more interesting than that. Even Buddhism isn't as interesting as that. At 6 p.m. I do my chanting and meditation till nine or ten then I go to bed. In Buddhism we recognize that the fundamental nature is always awake and that sleep is a kind of medicine for the body. The striker in our temple wind chimes is a fish, because a fish never sleeps. It's not the end of the day because there is no end to the day. **There is no end and no beginning**.*

Temple and gurdwara

Between the stillness of Buddhist meditation and the emotional exuberance of Native religions lie the more traditional devotional practices associated with regular attendance at a local place of worship. It can be a grand building of architectural merit like Timbuktu's main mosque on the edge of the Sahara Desert in Mali, or the sacred complex of buildings that make up Sikhism's spiritual capital of Amritsar, or the breathtaking white marble of the Shree Swaminarayan Hindu Temple in, of all places, Wembley, North London.

Or it can be those lesser temples and gurdwaras, synagogues and mosques that serve as unremarkable focal points for whole communities week in week out and which feature in no architectural guidebook. There is a lot to be said for the ordinary and the everyday, and spiritual seekers should take care not to dismiss these often unremarkable places of worship in favour of a dramatic and exotic spiritual hit.

Take the Shree Ghanapathy Hindu Temple in Wimbledon, south-west London. There are hundreds like it all over the UK, from the outside giving every impression of a simple community hall on a suburban street, on the inside recreating the vibrant, welcoming and prayerful atmosphere of a South Indian temple. Going about its business in a discreet and unsung way, it has adapted over the years to the changing requirements of its congregation, moving from providing purely ritualistic worship to dispensing every kind of devotional, educational, moral and spiritual welfare the devotee could desire.

Although Hindu worship, or *puja*, begins in the home in front of a shrine to a family's favourite deities, communal worship in the temple is considered equally important. Joining in these services generates not only a sense of other worldliness but a great feeling of community and belonging in the here and now. It bestows on the worshipper a real sense of identity, banishing the kind of isolation that so bedevils modern living.

In the (admittedly grander) surroundings of the Soho Road Gurdwara in Birmingham the same sense of community is to be found among all the Sikh worshippers there. Hymns are sung, prayers are said, births, deaths and marriages are marked and all are welcome, Sikh and non-Sikh alike. The community feel is nowhere felt more joyfully than in the *langar*, the bustling communal kitchen dispensing food free of charge. Look round and you will see young and old, women and men rolling their sleeves up and preparing the most delicious meals, all the while catching up on the latest news from their friends and families.

Stepping into these temples and gurdwaras is to travel back in time to a simpler and more caring era when entire communities were nourished and supported by faith.

Friday, Saturday or Sunday

The places of worship used by the three Abrahamic faiths – Judaism, Christianity and Islam – similarly function as community, education and welfare centres underpinned by religious devotion. But even if you're unfamiliar with the architecture you couldn't fail to recognize in both the grandest or the lowliest synagogue, church or mosque the devotional fixed points that mark these buildings out as special.

Dominating the synagogue interior, for example, is the Ark containing the Torah, the first five books of the Hebrew Bible handwritten on parchment scrolls. Invariably, even in the most straightened of congregations, these are housed in richly embroidered coverings topped by elaborate bells and finials to show the honoured place they hold in Jewish religious life. There is also the *bimah*, or raised lectern from which the Torah portion will be read – sometimes in the original Hebrew, sometimes in English translation. The interior may boast ornate furnishings such as elaborate candlesticks and finely carved seating but it will contain no representational decoration for fear of transgressing the commandment forbidding graven imagery.

If you're new to all this you'll have to decide whether the Orthodox or the Progressive tradition of Judaism is for you. The Orthodox is more, er, orthodox in its belief in the timeless and never-changing nature of the scriptures while the Progressive is more accommodating to the evolving insights of contemporary society. So, for example, expect black looks from the rabbi if you turn up on Saturday for the Sabbath service in your car. Either that or park it round the corner, as driving or any other form of work – even carrying keys or switching on a light – is forbidden. Useful tip: the rabbi will always know you've arrived by car ... and probably where you've parked it.

The Orthodox see themselves as being part of an unbroken tradition of Judaism that was forged on Mount Sinai when Moses received the Tablets of the Law fixing divine revelation for all time. Progressive Jews believe that revelation is a developing process that sheds new and ever-changing light on the human condition with each successive generation.

Christianity and Islam are no strangers to such controversies though. Islam, the youngest religion of the Abrahamic faiths, has not yet had its Reformation and Enlightenment and is only now beginning to confront such debates from within its own ranks. As yet these debates are still in their infancy. But in Christianity such debates determine the character of the worship you will encounter in different churches up and down the country.

At any given Sunday service you may find singing or silence, organ and choir, or guitar, keyboards and drums. Readings may be in the sonorous words of the 400-year-old King James Bible or they may be in the familiar language of the everyday. Dark suits and white shirts may be worn by the men in one church, while in another they're all in jeans and T-shirts. Some will be tolerant of homosexual practice; others will think it a sin. Some will be in favour of women priests, others will be vehemently opposed. And so on and so on.

By contrast, Muslim worship is remarkably uniform. Women and men arrive for Friday prayers by separate doors and worship in separate spaces (as in Orthodox Jewish practice), and the attitudes of prayer are well defined. Everything from the pre-worship ablutions to the recitations, the bowings and the kneelings is fixed and, once learned, require no intervention or supervision by a priestly third party. The encounter is directly between the people and their God.

You may not find such everyday devotions to your liking. They may even seem a little boring to your tastes as a seeker of spiritual experiences. But in their very regularity such practices have shaped men and women down the centuries as they have, in Eliot's words, knelt 'where prayer has been valid' and waited patiently for the divine presence to settle upon them.

There's almost certainly a synagogue, church, or mosque within a short distance from you, wherever you happen to live in Britain. Who knows, pushing on one of these familiar but unopened doors might be an adventure into a mystery – the mystery of faith that lies behind the mundane and the everyday. And it won't cost you a bean.

1 At joint number one, two traditions at opposite ends of the devotional spectrum – **Buddhism** and **black Pentecostal Christianity** (preferably with a good gospel choir). The first for its silence and stillness and for its detachment from the illusions of this world and the second for its noise and colour and for its unashamed emotional exuberance.

2 Likewise at joint number three, two strangely similar forms of devotion drawn from two different religious traditions – the haunting devotional worship of the **Taizé Christian** monastic community and the incantatory atmosphere of **Sufi Islamic** mysticism. Both combine utmost simplicity with utmost emotional involvement.

Melanesian Christian worship for its astonishing choral singing. Check out film-maker Terence Malick's 1998 masterpiece *The Thin Red Line* if you want to be blown away by the choirs.

13

Ethics and social justice

Love thy neighbour

If you're looking for a religion in which to exercise your social conscience, the good news is that you can't really go wrong whichever way you jump.

The fundamental teaching of all the world's faiths is to serve God (in the Buddhist case the *dharma*) and to serve your fellow human beings. In the majestic words of 1 Corinthians 13:13 in the New Testament:

> And though I have the gift of prophecy and understand all mysteries, and all knowledge; and though I have all faith that I could remove mountains, and have not love, I am nothing.

Other phrases such as 'no man is an island', or 'love thy neighbour as thyself' encapsulate the principle of altruism to which love of God automatically commits the believer.

You could, of course, do good works and not believe in God at all (you don't have to be religious to be good), but once you go down the religious route you will be taking on binding obligations to care for more than just yourself. Well done for giving it a shot.

In Judaism, you will be subscribing to the concept of *tzedakah*, or charity, which is considered to be an essential of the spiritual life. Judaism is nothing if not a this-worldly religion with rituals that relate directly to everyday life. The great thirteenth-century Jewish sage Maimonides codified charitable giving and broke it down into several categories. Giving money to those in need, he said, was good. Giving money anonymously was better. But best of all was to give practical help in the form of a gift, a loan or, especially, a job to enable the needy to support themselves. It was said that money handed over as *tzedakah* was never yours in the first place but, rather, had always belonged to the recipient.

But social justice goes deeper than mere personal charity (honourable though that is). It has its roots in the words and deeds of the towering Prophets of the Hebrew Bible whose uncomfortable pronouncements and fearless, thundering rebukes held kings to account and insisted that divine justice should guide the operation of temporal power.

When a group of young Canadian Jews took to the streets of Montreal, for example, to protest against the Israeli bombardment and occupation of Gaza in 2008 they were in a direct line of social criticism stretching back to Elijah and Isaiah over two thousand years ago. Their demonstration did not make them popular with the Israeli government; it did not make them popular with their right-wing co-religionists but their religion and their social conscience impelled them to protest anyway.

Becoming a Jew commits you to the principle of *tikkun olam*, or repairing the world and making it a better place than it was before you came into it. Loyalty to your country, loyalty to your community, loyalty to your religion are fine and noble things but they will always be trumped by faithfulness to God and to God's eternal teachings. It means you'll occasionally have to break ranks with your fellow Jews and maybe also your friends to stand up for what you believe is right. As the Prophets knew from personal experience, it is an uncomfortable place to stand – as you, too, might find out sooner than you think.

Christianity and the incarnation

Subscribing to the Christian faith will also commit you to more than just personal charitable giving. Belief in the Incarnation, that God came into the world in the person of

Jesus Christ and that the divine plan for humanity 'became flesh and dwelt among us', will not be for you a remote and arcane element of theology. It has profound implications for how you will lead your life.

Historically, it has inspired men such as William Wilberforce to campaign for the abolition of the transatlantic slave trade in the eighteenth century (in the same way that it inspired British upper-class women of the time to boycott sugar imported from the slave plantations in the West Indies). Socially conservative and distrusted by many Evangelical radicals at the time, Wilberforce nonetheless embodied the conviction that to be a Christian meant to put one's faith into practice in both private and public life. The sugar boycott may have been a minor act of rebellion in the greater scheme of things but it sprang from the same convictions.

Fast-forward two centuries and the faith inspired Martin Luther King to lead the Civil Rights Movement and to press for an end to segregation between the races and the oppression of black people. Though it was a political movement it was also a moral and religious one, deriving power from biblical principle and the example of Jesus of Nazareth.

Incarnational theology lies behind every aspect of Christian social teaching and underpins everything from the proper treatment of the poor to the care of animals. As a Christian you can expect to find yourself on marches opposing the proliferation of nuclear weapons, animal experimentation, the invasion of Iraq, or government cuts to welfare. Your new friends in the faith will almost certainly have been on demonstrations against South Africa's erstwhile policy of apartheid, against the siting of Cruise missiles at Greenham Common in Berkshire, or against the First Gulf War.

If you decide to join forces with the Methodists or the Quakers you'd better buy yourself a stout pair of boots immediately as you'll almost certainly be brought out onto the streets eventually in support of something or other – whether in solidarity with Zimbabwean refugees or asylum seekers threatened with deportation. Of course, you won't always see eye to eye with all Christians, some of whom will call you barmy or dangerously left-wing. Ignore them. Just politely agree to differ and reach into the wardrobe to fish out your anorak for another afternoon of protest.

Likewise, prepare for social activism if you decide to become a Catholic and to join a Church with a long history of concern for the poor and oppressed. That practical concern arguably reached its institutional high point in so-called liberation theology developed by Latin American priests and thinkers. In opposing state corruption and gross inequality between the haves and have-nots, it adopted a 'preferential option for the poor' and challenged the seats of power, from right-wing governments, to multinationals to the Vatican itself. It was criticized by many for being a form of religious Marxism and some of its priests were disciplined by the then Pope John Paul II but, despite losing the potency it once had, it continues to cast its light over the social conscience of the Catholic faithful.

Allahu Akbar

'God is supreme.' Despite its association with militant Islam and street protests against American imperialism, the phrase in itself is uncontentious and is merely an expression of how the greatness of God influences everything the faithful do.

Social justice is at the heart of Islam and becoming a Muslim will impel you to treat your fellow human beings (Muslim and non-Muslim alike) with equality. Islam teaches that all people have the same rights, privileges and responsibilities. The poor should not be exploited, the vulnerable should not be oppressed, and the weak should be protected by the strong.

As a British Muslim you'll be able to join countless social programmes and charities helping the homeless and the unemployed, working with children with learning disabilities, or administering rehabilitation schemes for those in need, from drug addicts to ex-offenders.

Charities such as Islamic Relief and international societies such as Red Crescent do not just help their own. Sure, they were there in Pakistan after the devastating earthquake of 2011 and they were there in Kashmir after the floods the year before. But they were also in Japan after its tsunami and in war-torn Liberia providing humanitarian relief for men, women and children of every faith and none.

Social action was championed by the Prophet, whose followers believed it to be a vital component in the building of a strong and mutually supportive Muslim society. You'll find that the mosque is not only used as a place of worship but as the hub of the community. Part social centre, part meeting place, it also acts as a shared resource for education, health care and social welfare provision.

The eastern traditions

The Hindu approach to social welfare and reform has sometimes been criticized for being excessively fatalistic in nature. Certainly the rampant poverty and widespread gap between the rich and the poor in India does not at first sight suggest a society based on care and concern for one's neighbour. A hundred or so years ago the situation was arguably much worse and it took the pioneering social reform of the Indian philosopher and economist B.R. Ambedkar to shake things up.

At the heart of the problem (for non-Hindus at least) is the caste system, which seems to trap people in a social class and deprive them from the possibility of movement upwards. Basically, society was divided into four classes, or varnas. At the top were the priestly class, or Brahmins; next the warrior class, or Kshatriyas, followed by the Vaishyas, or tradesmen and farmers, and finally, at the bottom, the labouring or servant class of Shudras. The more elaborate caste system, or jati, that developed from this classification has resulted in the so-called outcast or untouchable group called Dalits whose lot in this life was not significantly ameliorated by the knowledge that they were making spiritual progress.

Ambedkar himself had come from a low caste and had faced discrimination at school where he was ignored by the teachers and forced to sit outside the classroom. Even getting a cup of water required a higher-caste pupil to pour the water into his mouth from a height as he was not allowed to touch the water or the cup. Many a time he went thirsty.

What Ambedkar did in the late 1920s was to launch a series of campaigns against untouchability, eventually converting to (caste-free) Buddhism to escape the social shackles.

Becoming a Hindu in Britain today does not involve this sort of discrimination as the community is more integrated into western society. Often the local temple is a focus for welfare and educational work among the community.

Jay Lakhani, Hindu academic

*The more I dig deeper into this tradition the more I think it has a great deal to offer not only me but humanity generally. It contains this marvellous idea of **pluralism**, many paths to discovering the spirit. It is also what I would call **spiritual humanism**. As a true pluralist I would suggest to anybody that if he is a non-religious person, an atheist, he should become a better atheist. He should dig deeper into his own tradition. If you are agnostic search even deeper. You can only progress spiritually from where you are not from where I am. So if you are a Christian dig deeper into Christianity and understand Creation and so on in a deeper way. Whatever you do don't jettison your Christianity because that is your starting point. You can't be a Christian in the morning and a Buddhist in the afternoon. Be a good Christian, **dig deeper**. Dig so deep that you are almost Christ. Then you are there.*

Becoming a Buddhist will open up many possibilities for altruistic charity and welfare work. Here in Britain, for example, membership of the Friends of the Western Buddhist Order will open you up to a variety of social projects such as prison visiting, environmental campaigning, volunteering at hospices, working with those with HIV/Aids and so on. The guiding principles are compassion and the 'right thinking, right attitudes, right livelihood' philosophy the Buddha taught to his followers.

The Sikh gurus all spoke out against social and political oppression in their time and the moral legacy they bequeathed lives on in Sikh faith and practice today. Becoming a Sikh will ensure membership of a proud but far from insular religious community fully integrated into western society and working at all levels within it. The principles of altruism and social concern are reflected in their unique institution of the *langar*, or communal kitchen, which serves free food to people of all religions and none.

Ethics

Religions have always been concerned with what is right and what is wrong. However, over time our understanding of what is right and wrong has evolved and is still evolving.

When it comes to dealing with individual ethical cases there are wide disagreements both between various religions and within them. What an Orthodox Jewish community may forbid, for example, may be allowed by a Liberal or Reform Jewish group. Similarly, on many life issues the Protestant churches do not always see eye to eye with Roman Catholicism. You'll need to make enquiries before you decide which grouping is for you.

While disagreeing on the specific details and circumstances of individual ethical issues, all the religions agree that human beings have the innate (often God-given) capacity to distinguish between good and evil, right and wrong, and to make informed, free and conscientious choices about which to choose. On occasions, you're going to need help.

As a Jew you may turn to the Law and the divinely ordained *mitzvot*; as a Christian you may invoke the Grace of God, which it is in God's power alone to bestow; as a Muslim you may turn to divine revelation in the pages of the Koran; as a Buddhist you may seek the help of a *bodhisattva*, or enlightened being, who has voluntarily deferred his or her communion with the Absolute (nirvana) in order to stay in this life to help others spiritually; and as a Sikh or a Jain you may turn to spiritual guides and gurus.

But all the prospective religions at your disposal believe you have it in your power to exercise responsibility in thought and action and, ultimately, to be held accountable for them. Here's a quick thumbnail guide to what the religions have to say about some moral issues.

Capital punishment

Judaism theoretically supports the death penalty but in practice has made the rules under which it is allowed so restrictive as to legislate it out of existence. Such is the fallibility of human knowledge that Maimonides believed it better to let a thousand guilty people free than to take the life of a single innocent person. The State of Israel retains the death penalty but has not carried out an execution since that of the Nazi war criminal Adolf Eichmann in 1962.

The death penalty has both supporters and opponents within Christianity. Some argue that, while Jesus himself does not use violence, he never once states that the civil authorities are prevented from exacting the ultimate sanction. Others state simply that God alone has the power to take life.

Islam on the whole supports the death penalty on the grounds that the Koran clearly sanctions its use for crimes such as murder, rape, treason, adultery and homosexual practice. It maintains that the level of proof needed to exact the ultimate punishment for such crimes is deliberately high.

Buddhism has no unified policy but in general disapproves of capital punishment even though a predominantly Buddhist country such as Thailand retains it. Buddhists argue that a punishment of this severity will affect the soul not only of the criminal but that of the person administering the punishment, too.

Hinduism takes a broadly similar position, basing its opposition on the fundamental principle of *ahimsa*, or respect for life – even though India retains the sanction.

Sikhism is broadly opposed to capital punishment on the grounds that it is a vengeful action.

Abortion

The religious debate revolves round the status of the unborn foetus and whether it can be said to have rights equal to those, say, of the mother. The Anglican Christian Church views abortion as 'gravely contrary to the moral law' and condemns the number of abortions performed as unacceptably high. But it accepts that in the circumstances where the mother's life is in danger an abortion could be the lesser of two evils.

The Roman Catholic Church is opposed to abortion on the grounds that the sanctity of all life is paramount. The unborn foetus is a potential human being with the God-given right to life.

Judaism supports the sanctity of life argument but considers every case individually, not ruling out the regrettable necessity for abortion in certain circumstances.

Sikhism generally accepts that life begins at conception and broadly disapproves of abortion. Exceptions could be made if the life of the mother were threatened.

Hinduism takes broadly the same view but would mostly value the life of the mother above that of the unborn child.

Different schools of **Islam** take differing positions on the detail and circumstances of individual cases. They take the sanctity of life argument but accept that the lesser of two evils may be to sacrifice the life of the foetus when the life of the mother is threatened.

Buddhism has no unified view but broadly rejects abortion in principle on the grounds that it involves the taking of life, which begins at conception. It accepts that the life of the mother has equal worth and would go for the lesser of two evils.

Euthanasia

The views of individual Christians, Jews and Muslims differ on this matter. While the religions broadly oppose euthanasia and voluntary assisted suicide they differentiate between the taking of life by administering a fatal drug and the withholding of a potentially beneficial treatment merely to prolong life.

Buddhists, Hindus and Sikhs are not unanimous on the matter of voluntary assisted suicide but there is broad opposition to the practice on the grounds it is causing harm to a living being.

Contraception

Most Protestant Christian churches have no objection to artificial contraception provided that it used only within marriage.

The Catholic Church is opposed to the practice of artificial contraception on several grounds. The Church believes it is contrary to the natural law that insists the sexual act between husband and wife should always be potentially procreative in nature. Anything that interferes with this process is, from the moral point of view, 'intrinsically evil'. It adds that the practice reduces the essentially sacred act of communion between two people and God to a mere act of sensual pleasure and is damaging to the divinely ordained institution of marriage. Natural methods of birth control are permitted.

Hinduism has no objection to the practice.

Buddhism has no objection to artificial contraceptive methods that prevent conception (condoms and the oral contraceptive pill for example) but disapproves of IUD methods, which destroy the fertilized egg and therefore destroy life.

Judaism permits certain kinds of artificial contraception (the oral contraceptive pill, IUDs and, with rabbinic reservations, the diaphragm) but forbids the use of a condom on the grounds that it is wasting seed in contravention of divine law.

Sikhs sees no objection to the practice and believe couples may use any method of their choice.

Most schools of Islamic law permit the practice.

SPECIAL MERIT ★★★

1 The **Catholic** and **Anglican Christian** churches for their long record of championing social justice. Also for their institutional presence, via the parish system, in every corner of Britain. Together with other denominations such as the Methodists and the Baptists the faith has been the motivation for social welfare and reform for generations. In the nineteenth century Evangelical Christianity was at the forefront of national movements for change giving rise, in our own time, to such ideas as Christian socialism that have pressed for compassionate social change in everything from housing to employment, and from health care to education.

14

The environment

Awe and majesty

We could start with animism and end with Zoroastrianism (as most handbooks of religion do), but let's go really wild and start at the finish with the faith that defines some 200,000 people worldwide, the largest concentration of Zoroastrians being in India where they are known as Parsis. It's fitting that we do begin here because as arguably the oldest of the world's monotheisms Zoroastrianism also considers itself to be the first to promote environmentalism as part of its core beliefs.

Some four thousand years after its foundation it's still putting its moral authority behind ecological concerns and currently backing a campaign to save India's vultures from extinction. Why such a specific initiative when vultures are not exactly the cuddliest of creatures? Well, the answer lies in their importance (vultures, that is, not Zoroastrians) in the food chain. Until recently Indian farmers (most of them vegetarian Hindus) took dead cows to a special dump where the vultures would strip the carcasses within hours. The decline of the vulture population from an estimated 30 million to just 10,000 has meant that rats and feral dogs have moved in and begun to spread disease. So protecting the vulture makes sense as a form of organic waste and pest control. Neat.

However, the Parsis have a more personal reason for protecting the vulture. The community forbids the burial or cremation of its dead and, instead, puts the bodies of its deceased on wooden platforms known as 'towers of silence' where the vultures will take care of their disposal in their own inimitable way. By following this unusual funerary ritual Zoroastrians believe that the sacred elements of fire and earth will not be polluted. In this theology fire and earth are two components of the sevenfold creation of the cosmos, otherwise including water, sky, plants, animals and humans. As the only conscious elements of the created order humans have the duty to care for all the rest and, at the end of time, to return the world to its creator, Ahura Mazda, in its original perfect state. An overriding Zoroastrian belief, therefore, is that all these creations are interdependent and that the proper stewardship of them is a natural responsibility ordained by God.

If you find ecology interesting and important, joining the Zoroastrian faith would undoubtedly be a wise move for you – were it not for the rather inconvenient fact that you can't. Join them, that is. Zoroastrianism does not accept converts so you will have to admire their environmentalism from afar.

But don't despair. That environmentalism is to be found in other world faiths, too. In the Abrahamic traditions it's to be found in the Bible and the Koran and owes its origins to the overwhelming sense of awe at the majesty and beauty of God's Creation. In fact, in the Koran (40:57) humankind is secondary to the natural order:

> *The creation of the heavens and earth is greater by far than the creation of mankind, though most people do not know it.*

At a more prosaic level the early followers of Islam were desert people and knew more than most the importance of the proper handling of the land and watercourses to ensure their survival.

In the Jewish and Christian traditions both the beauty and perfection of Creation are stressed. Genesis 1:31 reads: 'And God saw everything he had made, and, behold, it was very good.' If you start with a divinely ordained plan (and a divinity capable of putting the plan into effect), you end up with a divinely executed world that it is humanity's responsibility to protect and preserve. At their best, all the religions hold the created order to be a gift from the Almighty, a gift not to be taken for granted or abused. In the pre-industrial age when people lived predominantly on and by the land the harmony between humans and nature broadly held. But a few things have happened since then ...

Dominion and stewardship

In 2011 the English-speaking world rightly celebrated the four hundredth anniversary of the King James Version of the Bible, a magisterial translation of the Hebrew and Greek texts that together make up the Old and New Testaments. Critics of the Christian Church's approach to environmentalism, however, point to one word (a mere 26 verses into the Book of Genesis) that, in its translated form, has derailed all attempts to formulate a holistic theology of Creation. And that word is 'dominion'. The 'offending' verse reads:

> And God said let us make man in our image, after our likeness: and let them have dominion over the fish in the sea, and over the fowl of the air, and over the cattle, and over all the earth.

Of course, good Christian folk have intervened to assert that this word 'dominion' doesn't quite mean what it appears to say. It means, they valiantly reason, 'stewardship' or the proper care for and responsible use of the Earth's resources. But too late. Too late. The damage has been done and the results of that unfortunate translation are clear for us to see – from the over-fishing of the North Sea to the industrialization of the farming industry, from the absence of cod at your local chippy to the omnipresence of burgers in the high street.

The ancient Hebrew texts had no such problem. Moreover, the subsequent four books that make up the Torah, or the Law, are quite specific about what human beings may or may not do with the Earth's bounty:

> If you chance on a bird's nest along the road, or in a tree, or on the ground with fledglings or eggs and the mother sitting over the fledglings or on the eggs do not take the mother with her young. Let the mother go.

So Deuteronomy 22:6–7. And what about this, from Leviticus 25:3–5:

Six years thou shalt sow thy field, and six years thou shalt thou prune thy vineyard, and gather in the fruit thereof. But the seventh year shall be a sabbath of rest unto the land, a sabbath for the Lord: thou shalt neither sow thy field, nor prune thy vineyard.

Just as human beings are commanded to work six days and rest on the seventh, so they are bound to work their land only six years in seven in order to conserve its goodness. Exploiting the land for maximum profit, therefore, is not only against divine law, it makes sound agricultural sense and is forbidden for the benefit both of humanity and of the Earth. Environmental justice is therefore a core Jewish value.

Though the word did not exist at the time, biodiversity was envisaged in these ancient texts. The extinction of species would have been a grave crime and so, for example, there is a solemn injunction against the destruction of fruit trees even in time of war. The natural world is a sacred whole within which humanity is expected to live responsibly. Leviticus and Deuteronomy often get a bad press these days and can be viewed as nothing more than a tedious list of arcane laws. Reread with the natural world in mind, however, these passages turn out to be surprisingly practical and in tune with the modern ecology movement. Think of them less as a tiresome list of thou-shalt-nots and more as a green manual way ahead of its time.

But, to be fair, Christianity has begun rediscovering these texts and adding to them unique insights drawn from the words, actions and teachings of Jesus as recorded in the New Testament. The compulsion to have mastery or 'dominion' over the Earth has resulted in the degradation of its natural resources and fuelled an increasingly acquisitive and materialistic lifestyle for some and lives of poverty and want for infinitely more. Christianity has been making amends for its sometimes unbalanced theology of dominion and recognizing that not only are there environmental implications at stake but also social justice issues. So, in choosing the Christian option, you will be joining a worldwide movement that has pledged itself to looking afresh at God's Creation and reassessing humanity's hitherto privileged position within it.

The influential Alliance of Religions and Conservation (ARC) has acted as an educational resource for Catholic, Anglican, Eastern Orthodox and Evangelical churches (as well as for many other non-Christian religions), which are beginning now to develop a theology of the environment as part of their overall mission. It's very much hands-on work, with churches and denominations signing up to long term plans with measurable and achievable goals in the field of energy conservation.

Should you be considering Christian environmental activism it's as well to be forewarned that there is some suspicion in conservative Evangelical circles, particularly in the USA, that you'll be signing up to a liberal or left-leaning movement. This isn't the case, as the people rallying under the banner of Christian environmentalism are drawn from all ages, classes and political persuasions and draw their inspiration not from secular politics but from the teachings of Jesus and the Bible. And they don't all wear sandals.

Islamic environmentalism operates on similar lines, taking the insights of the Koran as its guiding principles. Avoiding waste, pollution, damage or destruction is thus a divine command. Muslims believe that on the Day of Judgement they will be asked, among other things, to account for their treatment of planet Earth. Their approach is built on the concepts of *khalifa* (stewardship) and of *tawhid* (unity). Under the first, Muslims have been appointed guardians of the created order and should do nothing to despoil or abuse it. And under the second, the oneness of God is reflected in the unity of humanity and Creation. The Koran teaches that we should respect the Earth's animal, mineral and vegetable resources.

As a consequence, don't expect to be able to go hunting for fun (foxhunting and bullfighting, for example, are expressly forbidden) or to enjoy luxury goods derived from fur, skins, tusks, hide, horn or bone.

All the above, of course, comes under the heading of 'best practice'. Jews, Christians and Muslims all put the theory into practice to greater or lesser degrees and may even be divided over the small print of environmental theology. What's clear, however, is that these major Abrahamic religions represent billions of individuals worldwide and are often major landowners in their own right. The example they set in everything from conserving energy in their places of worship to managing their land assets with responsibility and care can make a real and discernible impact on the planet. By joining any one of the these faiths you'll be guaranteed to be a member of a global movement that can make a difference.

The eastern traditions

Hinduism derives its western name from the cluster of religious practices that grew up along the Indus Valley of north-west India from around 2,500 BCE. Those growing up in this emerging civilization were close to the land and close to the mighty Indus that watered their crops in times of plenty and destroyed them in times of flood. The inhabitants had, therefore, an attitude to the natural world based on love, respect and often fear. Nature had to be honoured and sometimes placated for it could bring contentment or destruction.

As a consequence, a simpler life, one in harmony with nature, is a condition most Hindus aspire to. But there is an inescapable irony to life on the Indian subcontinent in the twenty-first century – its drive to be a technological contender in an already technologically driven world. This has resulted in widespread water shortages, the desertification of many parts of India, and the pollution of the sacred River Ganges. There is great debate about how this trend can be reversed but some have said this won't happen unless the policy-makers rediscover the classical Hindu religious tradition of care for the natural environment.

In this they (and you, if you find Hinduism an attractive proposition) would be walking in the footsteps of Mahatma Gandhi, who embodied the principle of *ahimsa*, or non-violence to all living things. As a Hindu you would be prepared to accept that this life is only one of many (possibly many thousands) lives you will lead on the way to spiritual liberation. Your reincarnated self could return in the form of a human or an animal so there will be every incentive to treat all living organisms with love and respect. Coupled with the idea of *dharma*, or appropriateness of mental attitudes and physical actions, you will ideally tread very lightly on this Earth using only those material things you need to survive and those you need to help your family and neighbours. If you choose the Jain path, you'll probably have to consider an even greater level of physical renunciation, but the end goal will be the same – to develop a spiritual awareness that accepts the interconnectedness of all things in the natural world.

Shamasunda, Hindu farm manager at the Hare Krishna headquarters, Bhaktivedanta Manor, in Hertfordshire, UK

*Our farm is an ox-dependent, vegetarian farm. We believe that God created humans and cows in a **natural relationship**. That means they work for us and we look after them in return. They plough our fields and power our ox-mill, milling our flour and pressing our oil. In return we'll look after them for the rest of their lives – just like members of our family. Of course, oxen can't compete with tractors but that natural limitation of man's agricultural potential is what keeps things in balance and prevents us from consuming more than we need.*

*Krishna was a humble cowherd and fostered a **natural lifestyle** which we try to emulate. Being a devotee of Krishna reminds us that everything has been created in a **natural harmony**. God made it that if you farm in a certain way you'll be happier, healthier and more in tune with nature. We believe this is truly sustainable farming and it's proved itself over thousands of years.*

*We accept that some of our crops will be damaged by pests. The devotee farmer doesn't go down with pesticides and slug pellets to obliterate everything that walks or slithers. Instead, we recognize that in all living entities there exists that same spiritual essence. That same right to live. **This is a model farm with God at the centre.***

We read from the Buddha's early life that he left a privileged background to retreat into spiritual reflection deprived of all the physical comforts of his time. It's said he spent six years in the forest during which time he grew to appreciate the power of his natural surroundings and his intrinsic interconnectedness with the living world. He passed his insights on to his followers teaching them (then as now) to live a simple life hurting no living thing. He taught that there was spiritual strength and insight to be found in the *sangha*, or the community of ordained Buddhist monks and nuns. It was clear, however, that his idea of the *sangha* was much more encompassing than the mere walls of the monastery or convent. What he understood by it was what we've come to call the biosphere – nothing short of the natural world itself. As a Buddhist you will appreciate perhaps as never before what biodiversity really means – because you'll know you're part of it. You'll learn over time that material possessions are illusions and that greed and conspicuous consumption do not bring happiness. Be prepared, then, to be rowing against the current of the consumer-oriented value system of the affluent west. It will be a culture shock at first but Buddhist devotees say it will be worth it.

If you embrace India's most recent religious tradition, Sikhism, you'll also be embracing many of the ecological principles found in Hinduism, Jainism and Buddhism – respect for the natural world and a proper stewardship of its resources. As a practising Sikh you'll be motivated by a strong sense of equality that requires sharing and cooperation in all things. You'll learn that the tradition of hospitality found in the gurdwara extends much further than the local community. It implies an active rejection of inequality in society and a commitment to end the exploitation both of human beings and of the Earth's resources. As a consequence, you will see your ecological concern as a natural extension of your desire for social justice.

Taoism and the animist traditions

As a Taoist you'll be aware of the importance of the spiritual energy (*ch'i*) running through the natural world. Perhaps you'll be coming to religious Taoism from an interest in feng shui. If so, you have a heightened understanding already of how this living energy can contribute to your health and well-being. With this in mind you'll hardly be surprised to hear that Taoism's record of ecological awareness is profound.

The creative tension between the opposite but complementary forces of yin (darkness, water, and the feminine) and yang (lightness, air, and the masculine) is believed to be at the heart of the natural order. When these forces are in harmony countries, communities and individuals prosper. When they are out of balance unhappiness and even natural disaster can ensue. It is therefore important for you as a Taoist to practise balance in your own life, restraining excess and patiently going along with life's natural flow. As a result, you'll be striving for harmony with the natural world and will feel inclined to treat it at all times with respect.

If you're considering the practice of Shinto, Japan's indigenous nature religion, you'll be constantly excited by the energy and underlying spirituality of the natural world. A rock will no longer be just a rock, a stream no longer just a stream, a forest no longer just a forest. Instead all of these living things will be imbued with a sacred life-giving power that derives from the spirits, or *kami*, that reside there. Respect for the power that lies beneath those everyday landscapes will soon become second nature as you realize that forces that can nourish and sustain you can also turn against you if they are not treated responsibly.

The spiritual aspect of the Shinto tradition affects life practically in all sorts of tangible ways. As a result, sacred forests become sustainable forests and the trees that cover sacred mountains are responsibly treated. Plundering these sites for timber is not the Shinto way and the guardians of the shrines are working with organizations such as ARC to develop long-term plans to protect the natural environment in ways that are 'religiously compatible, environmentally appropriate, socially beneficial, and economically viable'. Not a bad blueprint for an ethical relationship with the natural world.

A similar sense of the sacred power that flows through the natural landscape characterizes the indigenous traditions of Aborigine, Maori and American Indian spirituality. Admittedly, it's rather a long way to travel but signing up to some of these beliefs would certainly be proof of your ecological credentials and of the seriousness with which you take your responsibilities to the natural world. Were you ever to go out hunting on the North American plains or in the Australian Outback you'd meet quite a different set of attitudes than you'd meet on a Boxing Day hunt in England. You would not be pursuing your quarry for sport but for food. You would kill only the animals you and your community needed for survival, and often you would say a prayer or perform a ritual of sorrow and regret at the life you had taken. In short, you would tread lightly on the Earth taking from it only what is your due and aware that other living creatures have as much right to residence here as you. A pretty noble world view, I'd say.

Closer to home, however, you might consider Druidry, Wicca or some of the Neopagan movements as religions that encourage you to put your environmentalism into practice. Respect for nature and Mother Earth is taken for granted and would come as standard with your membership.

Emma Restall-Orr, founder and trustee of the Druid Network

*What first attracted me to Druidry was its **integration of religion and nature**. It was **tangible religion**. It was **immanent religion**. Because the sacred and the divine are right here, they are able to be experienced without going through the medium of a priest or a text. The element of my upbringing that made most sense to me was that **nature is more powerful than human beings** and not something we should tame or control. It is something we should explore and learn about and respect. When we look at our body rotting after death we believe that a part of us is in our bones and in our blood which seep into the earth but a part of us is in the stories of our community and a part of us is in the creativity that we leave behind us and all of those make up our being. We're not contained in the physicality of one form. We spread out into **nature's consciousness**. I'm pretty much vegan in my diet and lifestyle so I don't have any animal products in any area of my life where I can avoid it. But now and then I'll eat eggs from chickens that I know. I know those hens and I know their song and when I*

eat the eggs I can feel the song of their living community. In
*Druidry there is **gender equality**. In fact, there is almost a*
dismissal of gender at all and an embrace of individuality.
Druidry is the only religion that teaches sustainable
relationships socially and environmentally.

TOP THREE ★★★

1 The **indigenous religious traditions** such as Aborigine, Maori, and American Indian spirituality for their respect for the sacredness of the land. Their material possessions are few but the spiritual riches they enjoy derive from a harmony with the natural world and are impressive.

2 **Druidry** for its worship of Mother Earth and its awareness of the energies flowing within the living world. Its celebrations of the seasonal cycle of nature remind all its adherents of the interdependence of all living things. You can't be a Druid and *not* be ecologically minded.

3 **Judaism** for laying down ecological principles three thousand years ago and codifying them into a system that has influenced Christianity and Islam ever since. Just a shame that Jews, Christians and Muslims have not always followed the spirit – and the letter – of the rules throughout their long history of both cooperation and antagonism.

15

War and peace

The dilemma

Step into London's Imperial War Museum and one of the first things you will see is a poignant quotation from the classical Greek philosopher Plato. As the founder of the world's first university, the Athenian Academy (itself sited within a sacred grove of olive trees dedicated to Athena, goddess of wisdom), Plato, we can confidently assume, was a smart guy. Smart enough for the museum to think that his thoughts on war would be worth pinning on the wall right by the entrance. And what did he have to say about it? Simple: 'Only the dead have seen the end of war.'

But wait a minute. From the religious point of view this is not so much depressing as counter-intuitive. Downright wrong, to be blunt. After all, the religions preach love and peace, don't they? Jews look to an era when 'the wolf shall lie down with the lamb', don't they? Christians turn the other cheek and Muslims invoke Allah as the source of peace. Well, not exactly. Or, rather, not wholly and not all the time. If they did, why would we have had so many religious wars in our history and why might we just be looking at more to come? Correct answers on a postcard will surely be rewarded with a Nobel Prize.

So if you're trying to find a path through the maze of conflicting scriptural texts about war and peace be prepared for a mass of baffling contradictions along the way. And before you decide which religion is going to be for you, you'd better also decide what it is you want.

Are you looking for the pacifist option, the position that says all war is unjustifiable and that taking up arms against your fellow human beings is always wrong? If so, you're going to have to prepare yourself for criticism. You may need broad shoulders to withstand the flak that could come your way for apparently sitting back in comfort and opting out of an armed struggle in pursuit of which (and for your benefit) some of those fellow human beings are prepared to lose their lives. It's a perfectly moral position to take, of course – and many religions and denominations do – but it's not always an easy one to embrace.

Or are you looking for a position that believes armed force can be acceptable under certain circumstances – sometimes for defensive reasons when the lives of your family and friends are directly endangered, sometimes for aggressive reasons when a tyrant or sadist is threatening a country, a community, or a principle you hold dear? This option will be an easier one to take since most religions recognize the moral and spiritual dilemma involved when a religion of peace is confronted by the reality of aggression. Some of the brightest minds have reflected on this dilemma and, working on the principle of the least bad option, have laid down rules to be followed and conditions to be met before a so-called 'just war' can be embarked upon.

What you're going to have to do is weigh up the arguments before picking the religion that suits your temperament and your conscience.

The scripture and the sword

The Bhagavad Gita, perhaps the central text of classical Hinduism, is set on a battlefield where Lord Krishna encourages Arjuna to find the courage to fight and defeat his enemies. The Prophet Muhammad was a warrior and saw his bloody victory over the Meccan population as an early confirmation of his faith. Sikhs carry a *kirpan*, a short sword that, it is said, once unsheathed should be used to draw blood. Joshua and David, central figures in the Jewish narrative, were fighting men of action. The Samurai, or warrior class of feudal Japan, were influenced by Shinto and Buddhism, which gave them a mental discipline to wield the sword with skill and not to fear death. It is impossible to read many of the classic religious texts without noting the martial imagery that is woven into them. The question is to what degree such imagery is metaphorical and to what degree it is a literal inducement to fight.

In the case of the Bhagavad Gita, Hindu commentators say that the text does indeed involve a battle, the battle of life, and that it does involve fighting over a kingdom, the Kingdom of Heaven. Arjuna, they add, though flesh and blood in the story, represents nothing less than the human soul.

But it is impossible not to be moved by the human dimension. When we see Arjuna overcome by despair before the battle begins, confessing to Krishna, 'When I see all my kinsmen who have come here on this field of battle, life goes from my limbs and they sink and my mouth is hot and dry. A trembling overcomes my body and my hair shudders in horror,' we are witnessing the terror every fighting soldier has experienced before the moment of engagement. This is the fear of the squaddies in the trenches at Paschendaele; this is the dread of the men in the landing craft heading for Omaha beach in Steven Spielberg's *Saving Private Ryan*. This is the reality of war and simultaneously a metaphor for another kind of struggle, one that requires every ounce of human courage and which recalls the words of the Gujurati song, 'The way of the Lord is for heroes. It is not for cowards. Love is to be won at the cost of death.'

If you're wondering where this would leave you as a Hindu called up to fight a war in the twenty-first century, you'd have to weigh up two apparently contradictory ideas. The first involves the principle of *ahimsa*, or non-violence, to all living things and the second involves a proper understanding of the duties and responsibilities of the warrior caste of Hindus (the Kshatriyas). On the one hand, you are not to take life whether on the battlefield or elsewhere; on the other, as a fighter, you will be permitted to use force of arms in self-defence. Even when the cause is just you will have to observe the rules of war by sparing the sick, the old, children and women – and, importantly, not attack the enemy from behind. Restraint, even in battle, is common to many religions.

The British Army is instructed to do similar things today. Talk to serving soldiers returning from Afghanistan and many of them will tell you that quite often they have been prevented from taking out a Taliban fighter even though his rifle is trained on their platoon. Why? Because the guy has conveniently placed himself behind a young boy and the rules of engagement forbid the targeting of civilians. Likewise, you as a Hindu soldier, will have to follow the religious rules of engagement – at whatever cost to yourself.

But Krishna taught Arjuna something else – and it's something you're going to have to get your head round if you take the Hindu approach to warfare. You'll be told that, in the end, it doesn't matter in the cosmic scheme of things that you lose your life. Violence can affect only the body not the soul and a struggle in a just cause will hasten your spiritual journey towards the Godhead. It may not sound brilliant on a recruitment poster but that could be part of the deal if you sign up to the faith.

Islam and warfare

In Islam (and in all other religions for that matter) self-defence is a justification for taking up arms. But such is the solidarity of the Muslim community worldwide (the *umma*) that war is also permissible against an army that is attacking another Muslim state or against a nation that is oppressing its own Muslim population. However, only the minimum force necessary is to be used and the vanquished should be treated with compassion in defeat.

If you are drawn to Islam, however, be careful about the mosque you choose to study it in. Some Muslim 'scholars' take a more radical view of all the above and take things several steps further. They use the Koran not only to justify a defensive war but also to sanction a war against unbelievers as a means of spreading the faith, adding that those Muslims who are not practising the faith properly (i.e. the way these 'scholars' would like them to) are fair game, too. They can be targeted as enemies of God and killed with impunity.

In Britain today there is a small handful of preachers purveying such a message and a small group of misguided followers prepared to carry it out – as passengers (some of them Muslim) on the Tube and London buses learned to their cost on 7 July 2005. The vast majority, of course, want nothing to do with such partial reading of the Book.

Before signing up at a course of study at these mosques, therefore, you'd be well advised to make a few enquiries. What exactly are the qualifications of these 'scholars'? Where did they study, just how good is their Arabic (and, crucially, how good is their English), which Islamic school of jurisprudence do they subscribe to, how familiar with the traditions of British life and democracy are they? If you're in any doubt get a second opinion – at another mosque not associated with that one. Above all, find a place that will allow you independence of thought and one that will allow you to disagree without thinking you a traitor or an unbeliever. Use your mind, your compassion and your conscience. No book speaks unaided. It needs a human interpreter and, as we all know, human beings are fallible. This incidentally applies to every faith you might be considering. Faith should not be force nor is it invalidated by reason.

The wars described above come under the category of *jihad*, or holy war, but popular misconceptions of this principle abound. Its primary meaning is the internal spiritual struggle of every Muslim trying to lead a faithful life in accordance with God's will. As with the Bhagavad Gita, the fight is a metaphorical one – a fight for mastery over oneself.

A middle way

'There is neither Hindu nor Muslim. So whose path shall I follow?' asked the Guru Nanak in the late fifteenth century before supplying the answer, 'I shall follow the path of God.' And thus, give or take a bit of supplementary detail, began the Sikh faith. From the beginning Sikhs were never a pacifist group. They believed they had to stand up for the oppressed, even if that meant striking the oppressor, since, for them, the moral duty to save a person from attack always overrides the moral duty not to cause injury.

However, as with other religions, conditions apply. The motive must be pure (excluding all thought of revenge) and the violence must be the last resort. Only when all other means have been exhausted may the sword (still worn today in its ceremonial form) be unsheathed with consequences that should not be excessive. In war, civilians may not be harmed and armies must be disciplined and free of mercenaries. Such principles have not diminished over time and, as proof of this, many Sikhs served with distinction in the British Army in the Second World War, realizing that the war against Hitler satisfied all their religious criteria for a just war.

The principle of *ahimsa*, or non-violence, is also at the core of Buddhism. Violence is in strict opposition to the eternal law of the universe, *dharma*, and is therefore inconsistent with Buddhist practice. This is perhaps best expounded today by His Holiness the Dalai Lama, who has consistently argued against the use of force by his followers despite the continuing violence done to Buddhists in Tibet. His message implicitly carries the teachings of the Buddhist sages down the years, who have consistently argued that non-violent resistance (even to the point of laying down your own life) is to be preferred to the taking up of arms against the oppressor. The argument goes that, while one Buddhist life might come to an end, the *dharma* will endure for eternity. Better, therefore, to die and remain true to the *dharma* than to abandon the very principle that supports all life.

However, if you reckon that you are not temperamentally suited to the non-violence and meditative self-effacement of Buddhist philosophy and prefer a more robust and physically oriented lifestyle, do not give up just yet on Buddhism because one aspect of its practice may be for you – martial arts.

You may know them already in the form of kung fu, kickboxing, kendo, karate and other more westernized terms, but they'll certainly satisfy any need you may have to express your physicality while still remaining true to Buddhist teaching. Your actions will be predominantly defensive and evasive, turning your opponent's wrong moves to your advantage or disarming him or her with the occasional paralysing grip, but you will always be trained to use the minimum force required to neutralize the source of attack.

From a distance even the average Buddhist monk or nun may look passive and demure but their mental training has taught them to be strong, resilient and impervious to the discomforts that would defeat most of us soft westerners – and, believe me, some of them (e.g. the Shaolin monks of China) are, pretty near literally, as hard as nails. They won't start anything but, if *you* do, they'll almost certainly finish it.

Judaism and Christianity

A constant thread running through the Hebrew Bible is the hope for a Messiah, an 'anointed one', a king from David's line to deliver the Jewish people at some unspecified time in human history. Although this Messianic age will usher in an era of longed-for peace, life before this mystical era will be an imperfect state of affairs riven by war and rumour of war. Jews have had three and a half thousand years experience of this and might be expected to know a thing or two about it.

The Jewish rules of engagement, while having much in common with those of other faiths, include historically one type of war that, if waged today, would invite (justifiable) charges of genocide. This falls under the dual categories of wars of obligation and wars of extermination, that is to say wars specifically commanded by God and to be carried through to the bitter end. In the biblical narratives laid out in the books of Samuel, Joshua and Numbers, the Amalekites, the Canaanites and the Midianites are to be exterminated root and branch by divine command. Men, women, children and even livestock are to be obliterated on God's specific instruction ...

Mmm. It does invite a moment's pause ...

But rabbis (in truth probably not all) argue that these battles are to be understood metaphorically, that one is to go to the absolute extremes to honour God and that what was sanctioned in the Bible's distant past does not apply today. To this the critics howl, 'Oh yes it does!', and point to the treatment of Palestinians as proof that at least an echo of this extremist attitude persists today. Look at the disproportionate Israeli attack on the civilian population of Gaza, they say, in response to the Hamas rocket attacks on Israeli territory.

To which the Israelis could reply, 'What is the proportionate response towards someone who wants to kill you?' The arguments go back and forth and are clouded, of course, by conflating Jewish theology with Israeli politics.

Either way, do not think you will be asked to obliterate a nation these days (or check out the credentials of the consultant rabbi if you are). Instead, mainstream Jewish ethics require a just cause, a plea of self-defence, and the exhaustion of all other diplomatic means before a war can be entered into. Civilians may not be deliberately targeted.

The reality, of course, is that, whether targeted or not, civilians will from time to time inevitably be involved in what is euphemistically described in all religions as 'collateral damage' and they will die – only then knowing, as Plato foretold, the end of war.

The prince of peace

The Messiah prefigured in the Hebrew Bible is believed by Christians to be Jesus – the 'Christ', or 'anointed one'. That he came not in splendour as a king but in vulnerability as a defenceless baby born of a woman adds uniqueness to his claim to be the redeemer of humankind.

The New Testament makes it clear that Jesus himself was unequivocally, in today's terminology, a pacifist – the ultimate pacifist, in fact, known throughout the Christian world as the Prince of Peace. But, although he spread the doctrine of peace wherever he preached, told his followers to turn the other cheek in the face of aggression, encouraged people to forgive their enemies, and ultimately chose the road of self-sacrifice in preference to fighting his persecutors, theologians have inferred from his teachings two divergent doctrines. The first is pacifism, full stop, or the *individual's* refusal to take up arms against hostility. The second is the 'just war' principle, which applies more usually to a community or nation state defending its people against aggression. The Crusades were arguably a glaring exception to this … but let's not get *too* bogged down in history.

Should you choose to become a Christian these days you can legitimately choose between pacifism and the just war, letting your reading of scripture and your conscience be your guide. If you subscribe to the just war theory you will have to satisfy yourself that war is justifiable on the grounds that it is confronting a greater evil, that war is the last resort, that all other political and diplomatic measures have been taken beforehand to avoid it, and that any damage done to life and property is proportionate to the righteousness of the cause.

The just war defence is probably the default position of the mainstream Christian churches (though individuals within them may beg to differ), but there are denominations of Christianity which, at no small cost to themselves, hold to the pacifist ideal as a matter of principle.

The main groups are the Anabaptist sects such as the Amish, the Mennonites, the Hutterites and the Bruderhof, who have been reviled for their refusal to serve in the military and whose moral courage, consistency and conscientiousness are not in doubt. There are such groups in Britain but joining them would require no small lifestyle change – including selling house and home, pooling all your resources, and committing yourself to the communal life.

However, if the pacifist lifestyle appeals to you, another possibility is relatively easy to access. You could join the Religious Society of Friends and become a Quaker. Not all Quakers would call themselves Christians but the New Testament ethic and a commitment to the social teaching of Jesus are generally shared by most members.

Mind you, if you join, you'll be expected to go easy on a few things (notably gambling, cigarettes and alcohol) and you'll not be allowed shares in the arms trade. You'll oppose blood sports such as foxhunting and bullfighting and not really approve of such things as circuses and zoos, where animals are exploited. It'll be taken for granted you won't wear fur and you'll probably have a tendency to wear sensible shoes, lots of knitwear, and warm anoraks – if only because you'll find yourself frequently marching outdoors on anti-war marches and in support of a variety of humanitarian causes (many Quaker women will remember, for example, camping out on the perimeter of the Greenham Common missile base in the early 1980s).

In return, you'll find that even the most non-religious of individuals and organizations will show you the profoundest courtesy, admiration and respect. Not a bad trade-off for the shoes and cardigans.

Other options

You might consider Rastafarianism as a religious option if you're looking to live out the pacifist ideal. With no central authority and no liturgical hierarchy, no one lays down the law about the official line on how to deal with aggression. Most Rastas are pacifist by inclination and would be unlikely to serve in the military. Likewise joining the Jehovah's Witnesses would effectively debar you from any kind of military service.

One of the first things the founder of the Baha'i faith, Baha'u'llah, did was to abolish the concept of *jihad*, or holy war. As a result Baha'is are for the most part pacifists who believe that world peace is an achievable goal. Joining them will ensure you a home among a gentle group of people whose mildness and tolerance of all religions are in inverse proportion to the persecution they have experienced in some parts of the world, notably Iran. Alternatively, you could become a Jain and live out the principle of *ahimsa* (non-violence), not just as a pacifist but in every aspect of your life. You may find it easy not to have to serve in the army but are you prepared to give up spuds?

You could also join the Ahmadiyya sect of Islam, founded in India in the nineteenth century by Mirza Ghulam Ahmad, which is largely pacifist in outlook. You wouldn't enjoy particularly cordial relations with mainstream Islam, as many Muslims would dispute that you were a true Muslim in the first place. However, you would be able to worship at the imposing Baitul Futuh Mosque in London, the largest purpose-built mosque in Europe – though the downside is that you'd have to get on the Northern Line and travel to Morden to do so.

1 The **Quakers** for their consistent commitment to the pacifist principle and for the level-headedness and downright ordinariness they bring to the cause. They're not ascetics, hermits or isolationists but are just like any ordinary man or woman in the street. They march, argue and demonstrate, but do so with a good-humoured and tolerant reasonableness that persuades by the force of its passionate humanity. They're old and young, black and white, rich and poor, husbands, wives, fathers, mothers or singletons, gay and straight, from village, town or city. In short, a thoroughly good lot of people to join.

2 **Anabaptist** sects like the Mennonites and Amish. Their commitment to pacifism and to any service in the military is principled and conscientious and over the years has cost them much in oppression, discrimination and personal abuse. You'd have to espouse the communal life, with all income going into a shared pot. It's a massive lifestyle change but in return you'd get security, companionship and a sense of belonging.

3 **Buddhism** on balance comes third on the grounds of its historic influence on Japan's Samurai warrior class. This is probably unfair to this most peace-loving of religious groups, but Buddhists themselves would be the last to complain. Also, despite the theory of pure discipline, spiritual focus and right intent, delivering flying kicks to the head and whacking people over the shoulders with sticks has got to be a *bit* suspect. Or perhaps I've just been watching too many Bruce Lee films.

16

Gender equality

The record's not great

Gender equality. Ah, yes. A short chapter. It's a tricky one, this, because, on the face of it, all the religions bar one score pretty badly historically. Though things are improving. In the patriarchal days, when most of the ancient texts were written, men unequivocally ruled the roost and women were consigned to a lower status in the pecking order. Authority and control were the province of men both in government and in the home.

In some ancient Near Eastern and Asian societies women were virtually the chattels or property of men, first of their fathers then of their husbands, achieving little autonomy as married women and consigned to the margins as widows. Of course, many women defied this arrangement and their example is wheeled out from time to time (often by men) as proof of their parity of status. But these have been exceptions. Overwhelmingly, for most of history and in most civilizations, women have been deemed to be inferior. In the context of their time the religions did some things to ameliorate the arrangement, according women special honours, privileges and rights. But the fact that they had to be 'accorded' these honours in the first place (and accorded them, of course, by the men who administered the system) rather than be entitled to them as of right shows how low the bar was. Only with the rise of feminism has that begun significantly to change – and in the eyes of many women not nearly enough.

Women's ability to rise up the religious hierarchy and achieve equality in ministerial and sacramental functions varies widely from religion to religion and just as widely within religious denominations. So any women considering signing up officially to the religious life should assess the level of their personal ambitions and aspirations and shop around for the system that matches their life plan. Expecting to be even a priest in the Roman Catholic and Eastern Orthodox Churches, for example, is an absolute non-starter for the foreseeable future but, with a fair wind, you'll almost certainly be able to become a bishop quite soon in the Church of England. Within the wider Anglican Communion that's already a possibility and in the USA, Canada and New Zealand the phenomenon of women bishops causes not the slightest comment or surprise. It might cause disapproval by a number of Christian men *and* women but that is another matter entirely.

Just not the same

The standard argument in all the religions is that men and women are the same but different (or perhaps different but the same). It is said (originally by men, who broadly made the rules, but also by those women who are happy to follow them) that women are the equal of men but that they are complementary to them. In other words, that they are to be treated equally in broad principle but differently in religious particulars.

A word about terminology first. Generally speaking the fault line in all religions occurs between those it's convenient to call orthodox, traditional or conservative and those journalists like to call liberal, progressive, or reforming. They're not always precise terms but they're useful.

Of course, all this starts at the top – with God. In the Abrahamic religions He is traditionally imagined as a man – variously as a Father Almighty, a supreme ruler and judge (roles only men could perform). When God makes His intervention in the Christian New Testament He does so in the Incarnation, coming to Earth in the male person of Jesus and not as a woman, which He could just as easily have chosen to do. Moreover, as His revelation unfolds it is announced to a succession of men. First to Abram then to Moses, through David and the Prophets. Unusually, it is next announced in the New Testament to a woman, Jesus' mother Mary, before resuming the pattern and impressing itself on John the Baptist, Saul of Tarsus (later to become St Paul) and, in the Koran, on the 'Seal of the Prophets', Muhammad and his successors. Not only is God male, most of those in leadership are, too. Contrast this with eastern religions, which boast a pantheon of male and female divinities but an essentially formless, genderless Supreme Being. Feminist theology is recasting the nature of the divine but the template has broadly been set.

There have been moves to rediscover the feminine imagery that accompanies descriptions of God in the Bible and in the works of Christian writers. The Prophet Isaiah, for example, talks of God being like a mother comforting her child and the fourteenth-century writer and hermit Mother Julian of Norwich refers to the motherhood of God. Some fear that referring to God as 'Mother' may sound suspiciously like Paganism or New Age thinking, while others defend its use as part of the ongoing drive to make inclusive language standard practice.

Orthodox Judaism assigns different roles and religious obligations to the sexes and crucially does not require women to study the Torah nor does it allow them to lead prayers in the synagogue. It does not recognize women as rabbis, so if you want to study the Jewish texts to a high level in order to head a congregation, you'll have to do so under the auspices of Liberal or Reform Judaism (collectively known as Progressive Judaism). By way of a further level of complexity Conservative Judaism has begun to admit women to the rabbinate and allow them to perform many religious functions in the synagogue. Even so, if you're planning a future as a star within a Conservative firmament, be prepared to have to fight your corner. In Progressive Judaism most of the battles you'll have to fight have already been fought – and won.

Christian women, however, have been fighting for ordination to the Anglican priesthood for over half a century and, in 1992, secured a victory when the Church's ruling body voted in favour of women priests. The pressure's being kept up and now the movement is directing its efforts to securing the consecration of women as bishops. The message is: it's a woman's life in the Church of England.

Don't expect such a future for yourself in the Roman Catholic or Eastern Orthodox churches, where the sacramental ministry is reserved for men only. The irony here though is that week by week in Britain it is women who make up the bulk of Christian congregations, and in the Soviet Union pre-Perestroika it was women who kept the flame of Christian worship alive in churches that were otherwise destined to be museums.

So, if you're preparing to take on the male hierarchy, you'll need a convincing argument to counter those who maintain that women are debarred from sacramental authority on the grounds that Jesus and all his disciples were men. So here's one: Jesus' treatment of women, was revolutionary for its time (engaging with women as equals or helping them publicly in defiance of the conventions of the day) and instituted a radical reappraisal of gender relationships that the church has failed to build on. Here's another; the fact that Mary Magdalene was the first person to meet the risen Christ and spread the news about it makes her in effect the first priest – and maybe even the first bishop.

Although there are some who say that the Prophet Muhammad broke similar social conventions in his day to promote women's rights, the dominant view within Islam is that women have only limited roles in religious leadership positions. It's a fair bet, therefore, that you can say goodbye to becoming a female imam leading a mixed mosque congregation within the next couple of generations. There are liberal Islamic scholars and there are a handful of Muslim feminists offering a contradictory critique of a women's traditional role within Islam but their voices have not succeeded yet in changing attitudes that have been set for around fifteen hundred years.

Islam is not alone. Among those religious groups that do not admit women to senior ministerial roles are the Church of Jesus Christ of Latter-day Saints (the Mormons) and the Jehovah's Witnesses. Expect to go around in all weathers knocking on doors and dodging Rottweilers and yapping terriers to distribute the latest issue of *The Watchtower*, but don't expect to be a deacon or an elder in the JWs if you're a woman.

Other denominations, other alternatives

All is not lost, however, if you as a woman have your heart set on an ordained leadership role within other Christian denominations. The Salvation Army will welcome you and kit you out in a jolly smart uniform as well. The Assemblies of God, the Church of Scotland, the Baptist Union, the Methodists – plus the Churches of Denmark, Iceland, Norway and Sweden, and the Evangelical (Lutheran) Church of Finland – will also recognize your gifts.

But it's perhaps the Quakers (aka the Religious Society of Friends) who will see you as the equal of men in all you do, whether it is preaching, teaching or merely going about your business as an ordinary woman illuminated by the 'inner light' of Christ and requiring no clerical mediator to let it shine in all its glory. In common with most Protestant churches, the Quakers recognize the priesthood of all believers and recognize the humblest as the highest. At Quaker meetings there is no structured service so the ministrations of a priest aren't needed anyway. Instead, people wait in silence until members rise to speak as the spirit moves. But whether you have gifts as an administrator, thinker, carer, educator, social campaigner, or rank-and-file worshipper you will be valued as one among absolute equals.

The eastern and other traditions

Both men and women can be *pujaris*, or Hindu priests ordained to carry out religious rituals (*puja*) in the temple. They can also join the monastic community (the *sangha*) instituted by the Buddha at the specific request of his foster mother (good to know the Enlightened One listened to his auntie), becoming *bhikkhunis* and enjoying full parity of status with their male counterparts, or *bhikkhus*.

Sikhism, though all its gurus were male, regards women as equal to men. Women are permitted to lead services and mixed congregations, lead hymn singing and generally perform all the roles of the male *granthi*, or supervising minister officiating at baptisms, weddings and funerals.

If you like the idea of becoming a *miko*, a Shinto priestess or shrine maiden, you'll be joining a long tradition that began with young virgins being consecrated to serve particular spirits at a shrine. A shrine maiden would be approached for advice, guidance and fortunetelling and would go into a shaman-like trance to convey messages from the hidden spirit world – much like the oracular priestesses of ancient Delphi. Commentators say the role today is a shadow of what it once was with many women providing assistance at shrine functions or performing ceremonial dances. Divination skills may also be required. And you do get to wear an exquisite uniform, a red divided skirt over a white kimono (the colour of purity) with garlands or ribbons in your hair. On balance, rather more eye-catching than the Salvation Army issue of blue serge.

As a Taoist priestess you will also be much valued at the temple or shrine, where you will expected to perform elaborate rituals regulating the *ch'i*, or cosmic energy, and helping to balance the complementary forces of yin and yang for the benefit of both individuals and society. Gender equality is one of the principles of the Baha'i faith. Recognized as spiritually equal, women are allowed to take a full role in the movement's social, spiritual and political life. Zoroastrian priests are exclusively male but, as the faith does not accept converts, this absence of a career opportunity need not concern you.

In addition, those religions venerating the Earth Goddess and practising nature worship are especially welcoming of women. Emma Restall-Orr, who has taken the name Bobcat, for example, is not only a leading light of the modern Druid Movement, she is also recognized as one of its principal spokespersons. In her writing, research and campaigning on things such as the proper treatment of the ancient dead, she is proof that women are accepted at every level of Druidry.

African indigenous religions also ordain women and will accept you willingly as a priestess tending a shrine to one of the *orishas*, or spirits, and acting as a mediator between the spirit world and humanity. Likewise, the syncretistic religions that absorbed the ancient Yoruba culture, mixed it with Roman Catholic worship, and brought it to the Caribbean as Candomblé, Santería and Voodoo will respect your talents. Indeed, many of these religions honour women especially, prizing them way above men for what they consider are their extra psychic gifts.

All in all, the Vatican's loss may be somebody else's gain.

Home and domestic

In many religious traditions the home is where women come into their own, organizing the household and, crucially, rearing the children. If you don't much like this arrangement and if it smacks too much of sexual stereotyping, look away now – although in Judaism there is an honourable tradition of the woman being the breadwinner in the house (by virtue of family inheritance or business acumen), thereby allowing the man to study the Torah full time). Mostly, however, women in an Orthodox Jewish home accept their complementary role, keeping to the rules of ritual purity that forbid sexual activity during and after menstruation and require prayer and ritual bathing before physical relations resume.

If you choose to join these women you, too, will cover your hair when not alone with your husband and be told where you can buy the latest, up-to-the-minute (and very convincing) wigs to wear outside when you are not. You'll also soon discover that there are moves afoot even within Orthodoxy to allow women greater participation in worship and synagogue services. Just how much you'll be able to participate will depend on the interpretations of your particular community but you will be joining a movement that can only get stronger with the passing of time.

If you're thinking about buying into Christian family life, you will find a world by and large free of the restrictions placed on Jewish and Islamic couples. True, you'll find that some conservative Evangelical groups interpret the words of

St Paul strictly when talking about headship in the home. For them this is traditionally the province of the husband, not the wife, who will have promised at the wedding service to love and, crucially, to obey him. But you will not be required to cover your hair or sit apart from your husband in church. You will be allowed to sing in the choir, run the youth group, read the lesson, and preach from the pulpit to mixed congregations. Outside strict Evangelical churches no one will be surprised if you choose to leave the children with child minders or relatives while you pursue an independent career. In short, you'll be able to live your life pretty much as you please in an equal partnership with your husband and with your own autonomous identity.

Though Islam in principle grants equal rights and responsibilities to men and women (and historically extended women's ownership and sexual rights), many argue that in practice the woman is effectively subservient to the man. How much is cultural (and can be changed) and how much is theologically binding (and therefore cannot) is currently the subject of much debate by scholars and the emerging generation of Muslim feminists. It is frequently pointed out that the Prophet's first wife was a very successful businesswoman.

In very conservative societies women's education is frowned on, independent careers are discouraged and even such things as driving a car is not permitted. Women are predominantly confined to the home and unable to go out unless in the company of their husband or a close male relative.

As a Hindu woman living in Britain you're likely to be allowed more freedom than you would have enjoyed, say, in an Indian village in previous generations. For one thing the size of your house or flat is going to mean that the traditional extended family all living together under one roof will not be practical. As a result, you won't be subject to the day-to-day hierarchy of relationships and won't be dependent on the senior woman in the household making all the domestic decisions – from the buying of clothes to the cooking of food. As you are educated, you will be able to earn your own living and have your own bank account. Your marriage will almost certainly be arranged but you'll be able to have some say in the choice of your eventual partner.

Sikh women have historically enjoyed parity of religious status with men and from the earliest foundations of the faith in the fifteenth century CE have been accorded greater protection and freedom than their Hindu and Muslim sisters enjoyed. Guru Nanak was distressed by the practices of the time that banned widows from remarrying (in some cases expecting them to sacrifice themselves on their husband's funeral pyre in a ritual known as *sati*). He decreed that Sikh women should not have to wear the veil, should be educated as well as men and that widows could remarry. He also condemned the widespread practice of female infanticide.

Sikhs today are proud of this historical legacy of tolerance and try to live up to it. Classically, marriage is an equal partnership of love and sharing between husband and wife. Indeed, the Guru Granth Sahib, Sikhism's holiest scripture, says:

> They are not said to be husband and wife who merely sit together. Rather they alone are called husband and wife who have one soul in two bodies.

In the gurdwara there is a natural mixing of the sexes that can lend a real sense of joy and celebration to the festivals and life cycle events such as baptisms and marriages. And should you as a Sikh women be initiated into the order of 'pure' Sikhs known as the Khalsa you'll be given the name 'Kaur', or princess, in honour of your special status, thereby taking your place as an equal alongside your fellow men given the name 'Singh', or lion.

Although Buddhism regards the monastic way of life as the spiritual ideal it also values the institution of marriage, within which women are traditionally honoured. So as a Buddhist wife you can expect the following from your husband: tenderness, sociability, courtesy, security, fairness, loyalty, honesty, good companionship and moral support. In exchange you'll be expected to show love, attentiveness, faithfulness, care for your children, thrift, sweetness in everything – as well as providing meals and calming him down when he's upset. Er, that's the theory.

By contrast your life as a Rastafarian woman (known as a queen) will be pretty much subordinate to your man (known as a king). And, perhaps unsurprisingly, the rule is that queens must look after their kings. So you'll principally be regarded as housekeeper and child-bearer. Don't expect a leadership role, don't cook for your husbands while you're menstruating, and don't use artificial contraception, as it's regarded as a part of a conspiracy by European colonialists to suppress the people of Africa.

For all the apparent flaws in the Rastafarian code of gender equality, it does have the virtue of honesty. Any of you considering a Rasta-based lifestyle change will now know in advance what's expected of you. However, it's worthwhile pointing out (as many women do) that what the other religions say in theory doesn't always happen in practice. Whatever the religions say at an official level and whatever safeguards are enshrined in the various scriptures, gender imbalances do happen – if only because no religious system is immune from the kind of sexism that has dogged the human race for rather a long time.

1 The **Quakers** (aka the Religious Society of Friends), who come pretty darned close to practising the male/female equality they preach. Women can be leaders, thinkers, activists, and spokespeople of this commendably non-hierarchical movement.

2 The **nature religions** such as Druidry and Wicca, which honour a 'Mother' Earth and to which women bring special gifts inspired by the Goddess within them. Wiccan covens are often presided over by a priestess, who is recognized as the most senior member.

3 The **Baha'i** faith for the equal role it assigns the sexes in both the religious and social spheres. At the political level women are also encouraged to play a leading role – for the rather magisterial reason that Baha'is believe there will be no peace in world affairs without the active participation of women.

17

Death and the afterlife

Everlasting life – would you buy it?

Arguably the biggest gripe the non-religious have with their religious counterparts is the latter's stubborn refusal to believe that this life is all there is. They take the poet Philip Larkin's view that religion is merely a fiction 'created to pretend we never die' and dismiss most believers as credulous fantasists who want the world to be the way they want it to be rather than the way it is.

To be fair to the critics, religious people do have form on this one. Go back to the ancient Egyptians if you want proof of the persistence of belief in an afterlife. Their elaborately painted 'Books of the Dead', drawn up by the high priests of Isis and Osiris *et al.*, contained a series of arcane rules, regulations and rituals the dead person would need to practise if he or she were to make the perilous journey through the hereafter towards the final goal – a state of bliss in which they would reside for all eternity.

Some five thousand years after they were written these papyrus scrolls survive and are on view at the British Museum in London, painting an interesting picture in pigment and hieroglyphs of what the Egyptians' preoccupations were. What is at once extraordinary and yet strangely predictable about their posthumous travels is that, having confronted monsters and demons along the way and having undergone all manner of trials and tribulations, they end up in what is called 'The Field of Reeds'. And what is this field of reeds with its lush pastures and cooling waters, its contented residents and well-fed oxen ploughing furrows under cloudless skies? Why, nothing more nor less than an idealized recreation of life on the banks of the Nile – *the very place they have just left*. Like humanity down the ages, the ancient Egyptians loved this life and simply did not wish to leave it. Their idea of heaven – and for so sophisticated a nation the idea is infinitely touching – was simply an extension of this life here on Earth.

Although Shakespeare famously called it 'the undiscovered country from whose bourn no traveller returns', death has been surprisingly well explored by every world faith. Near-death experiences aside, no first-hand reports have come down to us about what awaits us on the other side and yet there has been no shortage of people telling us, in photographic detail, what we can expect.

Religious texts have confidently sketched in the physical geography of the world beyond and even taken a stab at predicting its ambient temperature. These descriptions have been further elaborated by priests, preachers and theologians who have used such specialist knowledge variously to terrify, unsettle, comfort, cajole or instruct the faithful down here as to what lies in store for them up there – or, for those drawing eternity's short straw, *down* there.

So where should you look today for the kind of afterlife that suits your personal tastes? But before we list a few of your options ask yourself first whether you really do want to live for ever. You might think you do – on a nice spring day after a good night's sleep and a refreshing shower, stepping out into the sunshine in expectation of a satisfying lunch with good company, confident that money is coming into the bank and your career prospects are in good shape. Who wouldn't? But just say your joints have packed in, your bowels have ceased to function, your friends are dying one by one all around you, and the ringing in your ears just won't go away. Then what? Does the prospect of an eternity of that *really* appeal or might you be thinking you've had your three score years and ten and it's time to call it a day? All of a sudden eternal life doesn't seem that great a deal.

So before you start longing for eternal life, remember the words of the old saying: be careful what you wish for, you just might get it. Consider the prophetess of ancient Rome, the Sibyl, who asked the Gods for eternal life and was granted her wish. The slight flaw in her plan was that she had forgotten simultaneously to ask for eternal youth. So it was that she was condemned to age and age and never pass away. Then, shrunken and shrivelled, she was suspended in a jar until all that remained of her was her voice. When asked by jeering passers-by what she most wanted now she replied, 'I want to die.'

In modern times the tale of Nosferatu the Vampire (Count Dracula to you and me) sounds the same cautionary note. Ditch the Hammer House of Horror versions and check out Klaus Kinski as Nosferatu if you really want to see the world-weariness of the undead. Then ask yourself whether eternal life is everything it's cracked up to be.

So what predictions of the afterlife do the world religions offer and do they sound appealing?

Heaven and hell

Zoroastrianism, arguably the oldest of the world's monotheisms and currently practised by some 200,000 adherents worldwide, offers a vision of an afterlife based on morality and deeds done in this world. Accordingly, it is said that the souls of all the dead must pass over the Chinvat Bridge that stretches between life and death. For those who have done good deeds in their life the bridge is wide and reassuringly solid. For those who have done evil it becomes progressively less so, narrowing to the width of a blade from which all sinners fall into the abyss of hell known as the 'House of Deceit'. Those righteous souls who make it to the other side are welcomed by a beautiful young maiden (keep an eye on this theme, boys, it will come up again) and ushered into the House of Song where, as you'll probably be guessing by now, life is pretty damn fine, thank you very much.

Similar realms are said to exist in traditional Christian thinking, too. But to these Roman Catholicism adds a third – purgatory – where those who have committed lesser sins but who are still on speaking terms with God are sent in order for them to make amends for their wrongdoings over unspecified periods of time. There are punishments, to be sure, but those consigned to purgatory also have the hope that they will eventually be purged of their sins and make it ultimately to heaven itself. Before the departed prepare for life in First Class, Second Class or Steerage, however, they must first present themselves before the throne of the Almighty on the dread Day of Judgement when their good deeds and faithfulness will be weighed in the balance and tickets will be allocated.

Illustrations of what would await you if you hadn't come up to scratch were at their most graphic in medieval times. Those wanting a more modern description of the hot place, however, need only consult James Joyce's *Portrait of the Artist as a Young Man* to be given a concentrated three-page description of hell, its torments itemized in loving detail by the local Catholic priest to enlighten the young schoolboys in his charge. As a postscript to all this it's worth noting that some peculiarly sadistic medieval thinkers suggested for some reason (it's certainly not in the Bible) that the floor of heaven would be made out of glass so that those already enjoying their good fortune would be granted the extra pleasure of seeing sinners squirming in torment beneath them.

While all the religious traditions stress that the consequences of sinful, immoral or unrighteous behaviour are real, that reality is interpreted in various ways. Each religion has its literalists, who maintain that the physical geography of heaven and hell is exactly as described in the text. Equally, the religions include those who consider that the material qualities of both the heavenly and infernal realms are metaphorical descriptions of a spiritualized state of being that our eternal souls can expect after our physical death but before our bodily resurrection.

Islam is no different. In the Koran paradise is described as a garden in which those lucky enough to inhabit it are surrounded by cooling streams and clement weather, where they recline on embroidered couches drinking spiced sherbet or wine (forbidden in life but a permitted luxury in death) and eating their fill of delicious fruits and meats. And, with more than an echo of the beautiful maiden who welcomed the souls of the Zoroastrian departed, men can enjoy the companionship of 70 (in some accounts 72 or 100) dark-eyed virgins known as houris, or handmaidens, who will satisfy their every whim. Although the text tastefully refrains from assigning them a sexual role, it is a fair bet that many of the young men who have been promised paradise in exchange for violent martyrdom will feel distinctly short-changed if at least some sort of celestial hanky-panky proves to be off limits. Some of the Hadiths (the reports of the words and deeds of the Prophet Muhammad) strongly suggest the possibility of posthumous shenanigans when they confidently affirm that men, now miraculously transformed into thirty-year-olds who will age no further, will be given virility equal to that of a hundred men and, in one account, a sexual organ that will never droop during sexual intercourse. You have to hand it to the religious sages of every tradition. They think of everything.

The chief pleasure, however, and the greatest reward for the faithful is to be able to gaze on the countenance of the Almighty for all eternity – though, given all the other apparent distractions in the way of women, food and wine, it is not easy to work out when exactly they would have time to fit this in.

In all these pictures of male fantasy-fulfilment it is tempting to wonder what sort of rewards lie in store for women. Perhaps to spare female blushes (or perhaps not) the texts resort to discretion and euphemism on this one. It is left to the Koran to say only that men *and* women will be equal in their enjoyment of the bliss that awaits the humble and righteous in paradise. Given the questions that arise when such details are described in material terms, it is perhaps not surprising that many modern scholars prefer the metaphorical interpretation of the literal text and suggest that the sensual luxury described is merely a metaphor for the bliss that accompanies final unity with God.

Should heterosexual men reading this be considering the Islamic paradise to be a rather good deal, they would be well advised to do a cost–benefit analysis first of all. Access to these beautiful handmaidens is far from automatic. A disciplined life of five-times-daily prayer, fasting, total abstention from alcohol and narcotics, sexual continence within marriage (and no sex outside it), plus pilgrimage, charitable giving and an altogether moral life, treating your neighbour with kindness and respect, are required before you qualify. And, for those falling seriously short of God's laws, a quite different eternity is promised. And not, unsurprisingly, a very enviable one.

The Islamic concept of hell pulls no punches. Traditional Islamic teaching portrays it as a dismal place of dark smoke and eternal fire where the souls of the damned are tortured for all time. To ensure that the torments last for ever, the damned are helpfully provided with new skins to replace the old when these have become scorched by an unbearable heat which nonetheless has to be borne for all time. No cool water here to quench the thirst. Instead, boiling water to scald the throat, bubbling pitch and sulphur to torment the body, and temperatures well above the seasonal average to make sure your stay (a mere eternity) is not a pleasant experience at all.

In this respect the literal versions of hell in both Christianity and Islam are strikingly similar and the sermon delivered by the priest in Joyce's *Portrait of the Artist* could equally well have been delivered by a fire-and-brimstone imam in full flow. In fact, as you read this, somewhere in the world from Arkansas to Islamabad, from Lagos to Tooting Broadway, just such a sermon is probably being preached right now to rapt congregations of many different religions, convinced that they're ultimately heading for one of two celestial destinations when this life comes to an end.

There is one chink of light in this gloomy picture of hell and damnation. It's a strain of theological thinking that asserts that hell's punishments may not be eternal after all. It goes roughly as follows. The notion of eternal damnation and the word hell itself both derive from the word 'Gehenna', a smouldering rubbish tip outside ancient Jerusalem's city walls (for extra diabolical effect it was also said to have been used for pagan child sacrifice in earlier times). The fires of Gehenna, continually burning day and night as more rubbish and more human remains were piled on, conjured up a popular vision of everlasting damnation. But while the fires may have seemed eternal, the rubbish and human remains were not. These would have been consumed quite quickly. In the same way after a relatively brief contact with the flames of hellfire the souls of sinners would simply be consumed, leaving nothing left to be tormented in eternity. Punishment would therefore amount to the realization that their lost souls would be forever separated from God. Extinction would follow. Not a pleasant prospect, to be sure, but a sight less sadistic than the alternative. They would simply cease to be.

But if even this fails to still your reservations over (not to say abject terror of) what may await you after death, turn your thoughts for a moment to Judaism, which offers an altogether more relaxed take on the afterlife. Aside from the more esoteric strands of Jewish mystical thought contained, say, in the Kabbalah (so beloved of Madonna and other celebrity adherents), Judaism has very little to say on the nature of the afterlife. There are some allusions to the nature of heaven – an eternal Shabbat, or Sabbath day, for example, when all is rest and harmony, or, in an image that may have only limited appeal these days, an eternity devoted to discussing the finer points of Jewish law with Moses himself. Some lawyers may find the latter prospect exciting (especially, perhaps, if they're still allowed to charge by the hour) but for most of us what's attractive about the Jewish perspective is its refusal to be categorical about what follows death. Instead, it's much more focused on the here and now. It's enough to say that goodness in *this* life is what matters and that virtue is its own reward while we are on Earth. True, it assumes that any world to come will be a spiritualized realm devoid of bodily resurrection but it largely avoids too much speculation about the demonstrably unknown.

It is also true that Judaism has extensive and well-prescribed mourning rituals (it's said, for instance, that the soul takes 11 months to be purified after death and the memorial prayer, the Kaddish, is recited weekly for 11 months), but even here it's hard to avoid the conclusion that prayers are as much for the living as for the dead. The Kaddish is, after all, a prayer of thanksgiving and praise that expresses a yearning for God's kingdom to be established here on Earth. The New Jerusalem, Judaism seems to be saying, is to be built down here by the sweat of our brows, the strength of our arms, and the goodness of our hearts. Heaven can wait. Something it's well worth considering.

Sacred lands and spiritual journeys

The desire for some sort of permanent belonging somewhere seems deeply ingrained in the human personality. As we've seen, the ancient Egyptians felt it and so, too, do many of the primal, Native religions such as those of North America and Australia.

If you live in Sidcup it's probably going to be hard for you to empathize with the Aborigine tribes of Western Australia or the Northern Territory. But if you were to try you'd have to imagine that the whole of the landscape surrounding you was imbued with sacred significance. You would believe that all of it had been created at a time in a shared primeval past known as the Dreamtime. At death the true soul would simply return to the ancient ancestral lands of the eternal Dreaming. Admittedly the London Borough of Bexley and the suburban environs of the A20 lend themselves less to such imaginings than the mysterious, red ochre, sandstone mass of, say, Uluru, aka Ayers Rock, but the principle remains the same.

Likewise, residents of Tiverton or John o' Groats will not find it easy to enter into the mindset of the Sioux of Dakota or the Pawnee of Nebraska. Leaving aside the latter's historic propensity towards child sacrifice (reported as late as 1838), their idea of a blissful afterlife is to spend it largely as they had spent life on Earth – this time on wide open prairies where the buffalo are plentiful and where they can hunt in peace in the company of the Great Spirit Wakan Tanka. Their fabled 'Happy Hunting Ground' is therefore to them what 'The Field of Reeds' was to the ancient Egyptians – more of the same.

A similar aspiration drives Rastafarians, who make the distinction between an 'after' life (which they would consider a second-rate version of this life here on Earth) and an 'ever-living' life (which is this life plus a bit more besides). Not only that, anyone attracted to Rastafarianism has the added advantage of knowing exactly where they're heading for after this bodily passing. Not to some strange incorporeal spirit world but to Africa itself and to Mount Zion where they will live in freedom for ever. Let's face it, as far as final resting places go, things could be a lot worse.

The eastern religions, by contrast, offer a different take on the end of earthly life and see the soul's progress less as arrival at a place and more as an ongoing journey. To get into the Hindu mindset you need first to accept the eternal law of cause and effect, the moral law of the universe known as karma, by which the world and all living things operate. So be prepared for every one of your actions to have consequences. Good deeds and thoughts will speed your soul's progress towards the Godhead and bad deeds will hold you back (see this progress as a divine version of Snakes and Ladders and you won't go far wrong). But do not expect rapid results. Great patience will be needed since your soul's journey will not be completed in one lifetime. So, if you are thinking of picking Hinduism as your chosen religion, be prepared to endure many lifetimes and multiple reincarnations. Be prepared to endure thousands or millions of reincarnations until, through gradual purification and refinement in subsequent lives you achieve *moksha*, or release from the cycle of birth, death and rebirth, and your soul resides in the eternal stillness of Brahman, the origin and cause of all existence.

If you're thinking of Buddhism as your chosen world view, then much of the above will apply – though the terms will be different. Crucially, you'll be required to dispense with the notion of God altogether and to see progress towards enlightenment, or nirvana, as your ultimate goal. Only then will you have freed yourself from the twin snares of this world – desire and attachment, which keep true enlightenment always beyond your grasp.

If the idea of God is not something you can readily subscribe to, then Buddhism certainly has its advantages. But if you are heartened by the notion of the soul's gradual purification (in this life and the next and the next and the next), then Hinduism, Jainism and Sikhism could all offer you attractive prospects. Reincarnation is not always to everyone's taste (coming back as a toad or a flea or a game show presenter after all is far from desirable) but some religions (Neopaganism or modern-day Druidry, for example) take it on board as a necessary series of steps along the road towards an after world where all our souls will ultimately find rest.

And rest, finally, is perhaps the key. Not for nothing do practitioners of Haitian Voodoo fear the immediate aftermath of death. The soul, or *ti bon ange*, it is said, remains near the corpse for seven days and in this time is vulnerable to the malevolence of sorcerers who can impede its progress towards the ultimate source of divine energy and transform it into a zombie condemned for all time to walk the Earth as one of the living dead.

Night-night.

1 Judaism: Many years ago a friend of mine, a Catholic as it happens, was playing Monopoly with his wife and three young sons one rainy afternoon in winter. Between goes, the talk got on to the nature of heaven (the subject of the morning's sermon at Mass). The two older boys ventured their suggestions – endless school holidays, late nights, inexhaustible supplies of ice cream, that sort of thing.
But then the youngest, who had been mulling over the question with the utmost seriousness, interrupted to put them all right. 'No,' he said, 'This is heaven. All of us playing Monopoly together. Right here.' Cue silence and the dabbing of parental eyes.
And that's what puts Judaism at the top of the list. It doesn't presume to know what an afterlife looks like. It simply says we must do our best in this life and let the next look after itself. In the meantime let us enjoy heaven on Earth and our questions will be answered soon enough.

2 Christianity and Islam: The prospect of those houris is pretty enticing, it has to be said. So is the idea of a transfigured body able to enjoy the bliss of eternity with the source of all Creation. On the other hand, falling short of the ideal and ending up in the place of fire and brimstone for evermore makes the whole venture decidedly risky. However if you can bank on the prospect of extinction and therefore on the non-existence of eternal damnation, it might just be worth a punt.

3 Hinduism, Buddhism, Sikhism: Nothing better than rest at the end of a long journey. Be prepared for a very *long* journey, though – sometimes on two legs, sometimes on four or more. The, er, eventful trip will certainly make arrival all the sweeter.

18

Epilogue

So here we are at the end of the quest. Well done for making it so far. It's probably been a bit of a culture shock contemplating the strange things some of the religions might be asking of you. But here's hoping equally it's been rewarding to see what they'll be giving you in return. It is, of course, up to you to decide whether the trade-off is worthwhile.

There are, to be sure, many perfectly sound reasons in this day and age for not being religious. A quick look at trouble spots from Kashmir to the Middle East will confirm that quickly enough. But while there are many people out there saying religion is the problem, there are equally many sane voices of reason and compassion saying faith can also be part of the solution.

Perhaps it helps to make the distinction between what the religions preach and teach and what flawed human beings actually *do* with that teaching. There is clearly a huge discrepancy between the two. As we all know only too well, all the religions may preach love of one's neighbour and yet religious people throughout history have had an alarming tendency to do just the opposite.

Some years ago a cartoon appeared in the satirical magazine *Private Eye*, highlighting this discrepancy to perfection. The cartoon pictured a medieval Crusader army besieging a mosque in the Holy Land. A timid Muslim looks down from the minaret onto an invading force stretching back into the distance. There are catapults and battering rams, bows, arrows, spears and siege engines of every conceivable sort. At the front of this marauding army stands a fearsome crusader wielding a massive double-edged sword. He looks up at the Muslim and says, 'Hello. We've come to talk to you about Jesus.' Hilarious but sadly all too true. The humility and peace that Jesus preached is all too often pretty thin on the ground. Ditto the good intentions of all the religions when their theory is translated into practice and the rubber hits the road.

Judaism says, 'Welcome the stranger for we were once strangers in a strange land,' but a warmer welcome of Palestinians by Jews in Israel wouldn't go amiss right now. Christianity says, 'Turn the other cheek,' but Christians have at times been among the most enthusiastic warmongers. Islam boasts of the *ummah*, the fellowship of Muslims everywhere, the global brother- and sisterhood of believers, and yet the reality is that Sunni is at war with Shia and there are probably more Muslims killing Muslims right now than non-Muslims killing Muslims. There is a lot of denial going on in all the faiths.

The Catholic novelist and caustic humorist Evelyn Waugh once expressed mock surprise at those people who criticized him for describing himself as a Christian when he was so consistently obnoxious to everyone in his private life. 'Just think how much nastier I would be if I *weren't* religious,' came his mischievous reply. But of course such a smart alec response simply won't do. If religion is to be admired for its positive achievements, it's going to have to prove that it actually makes people better – not less bad. So is there any evidence that it does?

Well, actually, there is. Quite a lot, in fact, though none of it invalidates the good work done routinely by men and women of no religious faith at all. To repeat something already said: you don't need religion to be good. Many non-religious people are sterling humanitarians doing good work across the globe. But the fact remains that the practice of religion *compels* the believer to behave well. For sure, men and women fall short but their weaknesses and flaws should not undermine the religious system they espouse.

Look, for example, at the Christian institutions in the UK, USA and elsewhere and ask yourself how much practical good they have done over the years. In the fields of education, social care for the needy, housing, employment and much more they have tried to provide an often counter-cultural message to a society not always naturally disposed to helping the most vulnerable of its members. Then there is the formal network of parishes staffed by overstretched priests and unsung armies of volunteers giving generously of their time and money. One thing is certain, people would miss all that if it disappeared tomorrow.

And to the Christian institutions add also the Jewish charitable organizations, the Muslim, Hindu, Sikh, Buddhist and Baha'i groups working tirelessly within and beyond their own communities to make society a more harmonious place. Of course, to take two current examples that prove the reverse, there are extremist Muslim preachers who are doing their damndest to sow hatred and there are manipulative predatory ministers of other religions preying on children in their care and corrupting their innocence with evil.

It is a sad though inescapable fact that one instance of wrongdoing can overshadow so many examples of goodness in action and, in the process, can effortlessly fuel the arguments of the many critics of religion. Not only that, many of the voices raised against religion at the moment are extremely persuasive. The magnificent Christopher Hitchens, for example, routinely lays into faith with wit, charm, erudition, humour, eloquence – and a flurry of knockout punches. But where are his opponents? Where is a C.S. Lewis when we need one?

As we've seen, the ex British Prime Minister Tony Blair came out of an encounter with the Great Hitch bruised, bloodied and thoroughly trounced. We expected more from the maverick Orthodox Rabbi Shmuley Boteach, but in the end he, too, was floored in the opening rounds. Perhaps the writer and religious thinker Karen Armstrong would be a worthier contender. She's a brain box with every bit as much erudition as Hitchens at her fingertips and, as a former nun, knows the strengths and the weaknesses of faith better than most. And from the inside. Now that would be a heavyweight bout to book a ringside seat for.

But debate about the value of religion in the abstract overlooks what is demonstrably good about religion in its everyday practice. As a religious person you will never be alone. You will never be ignored or sidelined. As an old person you will be treated with respect. As a disabled person you will be welcomed fully. As a child you will be cared for. And as an adult you will be valued as the equal of everybody else. You will have an identity, a sense of community and a real feeling of belonging. In short, you will be among good people doing their best for their fellow human beings.

And, in the process of finding how you might fit into these structures you'll also find, perhaps to your surprise, that the practice of religion need not be a dreary chore. You can laugh with Orthodox Jews, sing with Evangelical Christians, meditate with Buddhists, chant with Hindus, and go on demos with Methodists and Quakers. Or you can sit quietly at the back of your mosque, temple, gurdwara, synagogue or church knowing you're among a community of like-minded believers dedicated to doing and (crucially) *being* good in this world – and just possibly hoping to be united with something greater in the next.

Index